A M E R I C A N ◆ C L A S S I C S

PLYMOUTH
1946-1959

Jim Benjaminson

Motorbooks International
Publishers & Wholesalers ®

To Connie. For Heidi, Kelli, and Jennifer.
In memory of Mom, Dad, and Uncle Albert.

First published in 1994 by Motorbooks
International Publishers & Wholesalers, PO Box 2,
729 Prospect Avenue, Osceola, WI 54020 USA

Motorbooks International books are also available
at discounts in bulk quantity for industrial or
sales-promotional use. For details write to Special
Sales Manager at the Publisher's address

Library of Congress Cataloging-in-Publication
Data

Benjaminson, James, A.
    Plymouth, 1946-1959/James Benjaminson.
        p. cm. — (Motorbooks International
    American classics series)
    Includes index.
    ISBN 0-87938-840-4
    1. Plymouth automobile—History. I. Title.
    II. Series.
TL215.P65B46 1994
629.222'0973—dc20   93-39571

On the front cover: The handsome 1955
Belvedere did much to dispell Plymouth;'s rather
staid image. This V-8-powered Sport Coupe is
owned by John Mitchum. *Finley River
Photography*

Printed and bound in the United States of America

Contents

Acknowledgments

There are many people to thank in the preparation of any book–and this *Postwar History of Plymouth* is no exception. Hopefully we won't overlook anyone.

First and foremost is recognition of my aunt, Clara Sloan. When I first expressed an interest in "old cars" she gave me a 1932 Chevrolet pickup–followed two years later by a 1940 Plymouth that had once belonged to my father (he was second owner, buying the car when I was two years old). It was that Plymouth that perked my interest in the marque and led to this *Postwar History of Plymouth*. I still have both cars (I got the Chevrolet in 1962, the Plymouth in 1964); today the Chevrolet is undergoing a ground-up restoration, while the Plymouth is maintained as a good original car.

April 28, 1949: The author with the 1940 Plymouth that he would eventually own.

Next is an acknowledgment to the late Don Butler whose book "The Plymouth and DeSoto Story" helped pave the way for this one. Many times Don's book came off the shelf to check a reference point–or simply to serve as inspiration. I never met the man in person, but our correspondence was lengthy and informative. Quite frankly, this book wouldn't have been possible without his.

Don Bunn cannot go without being duly recognized. It was through his efforts and encouragement–and his opening a few doors in the publishing world–that this *Postwar History of Plymouth* was brought to life. "Mr. Dodge Truck" was always there with advice, answers to my questions, and suggestions.

There are special friends associated with the Plymouth Owners Club that deserve special recognition. Heading the list is the club's current magazine editor, Lanny Knutson. Lanny's photos and comments appear throughout the book.

Joseph J. "Whitey" Eberle and Andrew G. Weimann II both deserve more than a pat on the back. Each dug deep into their extensive literature collections to provide research material. Whitey's dealer data book and dealer accessory catalogs proved invaluable. And I am proud to know that I am one of the few to whom Andy would entrust his fantastic collection of rare brochures and photographs.

Anytime I ran into difficulty I knew I could count on Loyd Groshong, Paul Curtis, Robert Semichy, and Earl Buton, Jr., to provide photos, data books, or other needed information.

There are others, of course, all of whom played an important role in gathering material for this book. Ralph Dunwoodie provided early information. Mary Cattie of the Free Library of Philadelphia and the late James J. Bradley of the Automotive History Collection of the Detroit Public Library were contributors long before the idea of this book ever came about.

Obscure aspects of Plymouth history came to light through the help of many people: Jeff Peterson, Bill Hossfield, and Channing Powell (Powell

Sport Wagon); Dr. Verne Clauusen (Walter Chrysler's birthplace home); Jeff Godshall, Frank Marescalco, Jim Russell, and G. Marshall Naul. James Wren of the Automobile Manufacturers Association (sales figures), Cathy Swartz of PPG Industries (paint information), and Columbia Pictures.

Library credits to the Automotive History Collection of the Detroit Public Library, Free Library of Philadelphia, Franklin Roosevelt Library, and the Carnegie Regional Library of Grafton, North Dakota.

This book would not have been possible without researching many books and magazines of the periods covered, including *Automobile Topics, MoTor, Science & Mechanix, Hop Up & Motor Life, Hot Rod, Motor Trend, Mechanix Illustrated, Ward's, Fortune, Northern Automotive Journal, Life, Saturday Evening Post, Floyd Clymer, Dell Buyers Guide, Motor Service, Automotive Industries, Automobile Trade Journal, Southern Automotive Journal, American Automobile, Speed Age, Popular Mechanics, Collectible Automobile, Antique Automobile, Cars & Parts, Special Interest Autos, Plymouth Bulletin, WPC News,* and the *Slant 6 News.*

Newspaper credits to *St. Louis Post-Dispatch, Tulsa World, Detroit News,* and the *Wamego Times.*

Book credits to *The Plymouth & DeSoto Story* by Don Butler, *Complete History of Chrysler Corporation* by Richard Langworth and Jan Norbye, *Life Of An American Workman* by Boyden Sparkes, *Standard Catalog Of American Cars, 1805-1942,* Krause Publications, *Chilton Catalog & Directory, 1928; War Production Board* bulletins, and the *Encyclopedia Britannica.*

Corporate sources included: *Ross Roy Data*

This 1940 lapel pin was part of the "Hotter Than A Firecracker" campaign.

Books, Confidential Bulletins, letters to dealers, *Plymouth Sales Promoter, League Monthly,* service bulletins, and hundreds of sales catalogs and brochures.

Last but not least are the many people associated with Chrysler Corporation that I have come to know over the years, including former and current employees: Madryn Johnson, Diane Davis, and Karla Rosenbusch formerly with the Chrysler Historical Collection; Bruce Thomas, Barbara Fronczak, and Brandt Rosenbusch currently with the Chrysler Historical Foundation; Otto Rosenbusch; Manfred Strobel of Chrysler Photographic; Marvin Raguse Jr., and George Stecher.

To each and every one mentioned here—and to those I may have overlooked (unintentionally), Thank-you.

Introduction

For nearly one quarter of a century Plymouth was this nation's third best selling automobile. When Walter P. Chrysler asked the buying public in 1932 to "Look At All Three" he was referring to Chevrolet, Ford, and Plymouth. During Walter Chrysler's lifetime, the Plymouth division of Chrysler Corporation continued to grow and prosper by building automobiles far superior to those offered by his competitors in the low priced field. During the bleak Depression year of 1932, Plymouth was the only auto maker to increase its sales. What we take for granted today was "exclusive" to Plymouth—all steel bodies, hydraulic brakes, and independent front suspension.

Following Walter Chrysler's death in 1940, a change came over the corporate attitude toward Plymouth. K.T. Keller, Chrysler's hand-picked successor, seemed to favor Dodge (the division he had run when Chrysler Corporation bought Dodge Brothers in the summer of 1928). But something else had also happened—the competition had caught up and even surpassed Plymouth. Stodgy styling, outdated mechanicals, and a reluctance to go "model for model" against the competition slowly took its toll on Plymouth sales. When Plymouth fell from third, it fell hard, dropping to fifth in a single year. Where it had once been the leader, Plymouth was now reluctant to even follow.

It would take a combination of things, including fresh new styling from Virgil Exner's studios and a V-8 engine, to turn things around. As the 1957 models made their debut, Plymouth was back in the sales arena as never before, breaking all time sales records in the process. But there was a dark side to this success. The 1957 models had been rushed into production and built in quantities never before achieved by Plymouth; quality hit rock bottom, leaving Plymouth (and Chrysler Corporation) with a tarnished reputation that would dog it for years to come. During the flamboyant late-1950s Plymouth quickly found itself "out finned" with bleaker days still to come. Continued unacceptable quality and outlandish styling nearly brought Chrysler to its knees.

Even worse, Plymouth always played second fiddle to its stablemates, despite its once proud record of being the Corporation's bread and butter car. Walter Chrysler's plan to franchise Plymouth to all of his dealers at the outset of the depression kept many of them alive, but in the long run, failure to let Plymouth stand on its own worked against it. Automotive writer Arch Brown once referred to Plymouth as the car that was "always the bridesmaid, but never the bride,"—a perfect assessment.

From the time of Walter Chrysler's death, the Corporation has had difficulty coming to terms with Plymouth's market niche. Even with the success of today's Plymouth Voyager mini-vans, Chrysler has openly questioned the advisability of maintaining the nameplate, though public opinion surveys showed the Corporation that "Plymouth" was still a viable entity. As this was written, word was that Plymouth will survive, becoming Chrysler Corporation's "value brand". Corporate "insiders" tell me "You should see what's on the drawing boards" for 1995 and beyond.

Regardless of Plymouth's future, this is the post-WWII history of America's number three selling automobile, its ups and downs during that critical period from 1946–1959.

Hopefully it will not only give the reader an insight to Plymouth's place in this country's rich automotive history, but also answer questions about specific Plymouth models. When available, comparisons have been made between Plymouth and its two rivals Ford and Chevrolet, including equipment and options, engines, transmissions, horsepower and performance figures, and gas mileage results. These comparisons are based on results published in road test magazines of the period. In preparing this book, production figures always cover the model year while sales figures from the Automobile Manufacturers Association follow the calendar year.

Jim Benjaminson
August 1993

Chapter 1

"Walter, You'll Go Broke . . . "

If ever the time was ripe to introduce a new car in the low-priced field, 1928 was the year to do it. From 1919 to modern times—excepting two years—Ford and Chevrolet held a one-two strangle hold on the market. Only 1920 and 1921 saw Dodge and Buick respectively bump Chevrolet from its traditional number two spot. But there was trouble in the Ford camp—old Henry reluctantly shut down the production lines in 1927 to retool for a new car to replace his antiquated but beloved Model T. With Ford's giant Rouge plant shut down, Chevrolet seized the opportunity to grab the number one spot for itself. Even after the 1928 introduction of the Model A Ford, Chevrolet still managed to stay ahead of Ford except for model years 1930, 1935, 1957, and 1959.

The number three spot has been more volatile. Between 1928 and 1970 that position has been held by Willys-Overland's Whippet, Hudson-Essex, Buick, Plymouth, regained by Buick, returned to Plymouth, seized by Rambler, then Pontiac, and finally returned to Plymouth.

For months Detroit newspapers had reported that a new car would soon enter production, taking aim at the low-priced market. As late as June 14 (the day production of the new car began) "Motor Age" was still speculating about the new car to be named "Plymouth." Who the manufacturer would be remained a mystery until the car's unveiling at New York's Madison Square Garden July 7. "We have named it the Plymouth because this new product of Chrysler engineering and craftsmanship so accurately typifies the endurance and strength, the rugged honesty, the enterprise, the determination of achievement and the freedom from old limitations of that Pilgrim band who were the first American colonists" read the press releases. Unruffled, Henry Ford told Chrysler, "Walter, you'll go broke. Chevrolet and I have that market all sewed up."

From Railroad Man to Automobile Magnate

Walter Percy Chrysler had come a long way from his birthplace in the sleepy little community of Wamego, Kansas. Born April 2, 1875 Chrysler lived in Wamego just three years before his father, an engineer with the Union Pacific Railroad, moved the family to nearby Ellis where Walter would grow to manhood.

Chrysler realized early that he had a passion for anything mechanical, so it was natural that by 1892 he was working for the railroad as well. As roundhouse clean-up boy he made ten cents an hour. Not one to complain, Chrysler did the job to the best of his ability. What the job lacked in monetary rewards was more than made up for in "benefits"—watching and learning all he could about what made the great locomotives tick. Eventually, he took a job as an apprentice machinist (his pay was cut in half—but it wouldn't be the last time he would take a reduction in pay to get a better job). From there he moved to machinist, then to general foreman, finally rising to the highest rank of all,

Walter Chrysler's boyhood home in Ellis, Kansas. The Chrysler family moved to this house when Walter was three years old. Parked out front is Lanny Knutson's 1949 Plymouth.

7

master mechanic. Bouncing around the country from job to job and railroad to railroad, he became, in 1908, the youngest Superintendent of Motive Power the Chicago Great Western Railroad had ever had.

He and his wife, childhood sweetheart Della Forker, settled into a comfortable lifestyle in Oelwein, Iowa. Chrysler's work often took him away from home, and it was on one of his many trips to Chicago that the hand of fate would point young Chrysler in a different direction. Visiting the 1908 Chicago Automobile Show, Chrysler fell madly in love with an automobile. Resplendent in ivory with crimson red leather upholstery, its siren song kept calling Chrysler back for "one more look". Before the show was over he knew he had to have it. The car, a Locomobile, cost $5,000 cash—he had just $700 in the bank.

After much pleading and coaxing, Chrysler persuaded Ralph Van Vechten, a banker friend, to loan him the money and the shiny Locomobile was loaded aboard a freight car for the trip back to Oelwein. Now all he had to do was tell his beloved Della what he had done! Relating the incident to his biographer, Boyden Sparkes, Chrysler told how he began to clean out the barn behind the house to make room for the Locomobile. When Della asked what he has doing he told her about the car, that he had "gone in hock for more money than I would make in a year" to buy it. When asked her reaction Chrysler replied "She did not scold me, but it did seem to me that when she closed the kitchen door, it made a little more noise than usual."

When the automobile arrived in Oelwein, Chrysler had the car unloaded, climbed behind the wheel, and had a teamster pull the car to his home—Chrysler did not know how to drive! Once in the barn Chrysler set about to learn everything he could about how it worked and how it was built. He wrote (in *Life of an American Workman*) "I wanted the machine so I could learn about it. Why not? I was a machinist and these self-propelled ve-

Walter P. Chrysler and Fred Zeder (front), Owen Skelton and Carl Breer (rear). *Chrysler Historical Foundation*

hicles were by all odds the most astonishing machines that had ever been offered to man."

For three months the Locomobile never moved out of the barn until finally, at the coaxing of Della, Chrysler announced the car would come out on that Saturday afternoon. Word spread throughout the neighborhood and a large crowd of friends and neighbors gathered to watch the occasion. As Chrysler recounted in *Life of an American Workman,* "The big touring car bucked like a mustang saddled for the first time. We shot forward; as some of the neighbors whooped and yelled, she bucked again and lurched into a ditch, rolled half a length farther and stalled, axle deep, in my neighbor's garden patch." A team of horses pulled the stranded Locomobile from the muck, and after settling with his neighbor for damages to the garden, Chrysler again mounted his great iron steed and proceeded at full clip out of town, where he narrowly missed hitting a cow. Making right angles at every section line, Chrysler made his way back to the barn where he and his neighbors pushed the machine back inside. By this time it was 6:00 p.m. He strode into the house, took a hot bath, and went to bed, exhausted by the trials of the afternoon—but Walter P. Chrysler had learned how to drive.

The Chrysler's moved from Oelwein in 1909 when Walter took the job as works manager for the American Locomotive Company. It was at ALCO that he came to the attention of James J. Storrow, a director of ALCO and former president of General Motors. ALCO had been drowning in red ink until Chrysler's take over of the locomotive manufacturing company. The Buick division of GM was in a similarly desperate situation, and at Storrow's urging, Chrysler visited GM president Charles Nash. Nash, a notorious tightwad, offered Chrysler a job paying $6,000 a year—half what he was making at ALCO. Chrysler accepted the job without hesitation. Arriving at Buick, Chrysler found a plant turning out forty-five cars per day. Within weeks, after revamping the plant, Buick was churning out 200 cars a day. By 1912, Chrysler was president of the Buick Division. In the meantime he had hit up skinflint Charlie for a raise—to $25,000 yearly with a demand for double that the next year.

Chrysler's stay at GM saw him rise to a salary of $500,000 per year, but he found it exceedingly hard to work under William Durant. Durant's undisciplined management style (he had founded GM in 1908, lost it to bankers, then recaptured it after founding Chevrolet and using its stock to regain control) was too much for Chrysler, and in 1919, at the age of forty-five, he retired.

Chrysler's retirement didn't last long—at the urging of Ralph Van Vechten, Chrysler took the reigns of the ailing Willys Corporation. His "inducement," as he called the financial package, was a salary of 1 million dollars per year with a two year contract. Chrysler's first act of business was to cut John North Willys' salary in half! It was at Willys that Walter Chrysler first met his "Three Musketeers"–the engineering team of Fred Zeder, Owen Skelton, and Carl Breer.

Political infighting at Willys caused Chrysler to pack up his family and head for Europe during the summer of 1921. He returned in time for John Willys to throw the company into receivership. Disgusted by the turn of events, Chrysler again headed for Europe, returning just prior to the Willys receivership auction at which he and the "Three Musketeers" hoped to purchase the huge Elizabeth, New Jersey, plant–including a prototype car they intended to produce under the "Chrysler" name.

Durant, who by this time had been ousted from General Motors a second time, had other plans, outbidding the Chrysler interests for the plant and the rights to build the car. Durant's third empire, Durant Motors, saw the "Chrysler" produced as the Flint. The Flint, along with the Durant and the Star, was short lived, and Durant's third house of cards soon came tumbling down.

For a third time, Walter Chrysler packed up his family and headed for Europe–this time to be called back to work his magic on ailing Maxwell-Chalmers. Meanwhile, Zeder, Skelton, and Breer had been hard at work on another new car. At Chrysler's urging, they moved from their New Jersey headquarters and settled into the old Chalmers complex in Highland Park, Michigan, on June 6, 1923.

While work on the Zeder, Skelton, Breer car progressed, Chrysler heard that Studebaker was looking for a car. Chrysler invited Studebaker executives to look at the new car, and the deal was nearly clinched when Chrysler told Fred Zeder of his plans. Zeder exploded, "Walter, if you sign that contract without my signature I'll call Carl [Breer] in Detroit and have every blueprint destroyed!" Despite Zeder's past association with Studebaker, this was one car he was determined to see built as a Chrysler. Chrysler withdrew his offer to Studebaker, and on June 6, 1925, Maxwell-Chalmers officially became the Chrysler Corporation.

Within four short years, Chrysler's empire included the huge Dodge Brothers complex, Chrysler and Imperial, DeSoto, Plymouth, and the Fargo line of commercial cars. In addition, workmen in New York City were building what would, briefly, be the tallest building in the world, the 1,046ft, seventy-seven story Chrysler Building (still the tenth tallest building in the world). Walter P. Chrysler had come out of retirement for good.

The Early Years

"Chrysler Springs A Surprise. Sets new style of 'dress' of cars–unveils the Plymouth, a smart new four" read the headlines in the July 7, 1928, edition of *Automobile Topics. Motor Age*, published two days earlier, gave the new Plymouth prominence over its parent, proclaiming "New Plymouth and Improved Chrysler for 1929." Badged as the "Chrysler-Plymouth," the new cars were slotted at the bottom end of the Chrysler lineup. Like Henry Ford's Model A, which "borrowed" its styling from the Lincoln, the new Plymouth looked very much like the Chryslers. With a 109in wheelbase, the car fell into line with the former Chrysler "50" and "52" that it replaced.

At $725 the Plymouth sedan was considerably higher priced than its rivals from Ford ($585) and Chevrolet ($495). Fairly conventional in styling, its "Silver Dome" 45hp engine was capable of propelling the car to speeds of 60mph. Improvements over the Chrysler-Maxwell engine included full force-feed lubrication, a special manifold, larger diameter chrome-nickel intake vales, crankcase ventilation, aluminum-alloy ventilated bridge pistons, silchrome steel exhaust valves, friction-type impulse neutralizer for vibration dampening, and an oil filter and air cleaner as standard equipment. In an industry first for low-price cars, four wheel hydraulic brakes were standard. Plymouth's six body styles were composite (wood over metal) for its first two model years.

Known as the Model Q, the cars were considered 1929 models by the factory. Q production continued until February 4, 1929, when it was re-

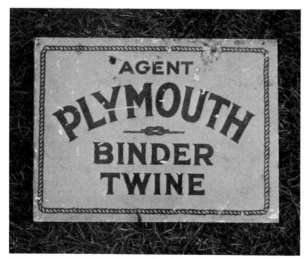

Neither Plymouth Binder Twine nor Plymouth Rope were related to the car company, but the familiar signs helped give the new car name-recognition, especially among the farming community. Richard Langworth, in his book *Kaiser-Frazer, The Last Onslaught On Detroit* recounted how Plymouth came to be named. When Chrysler's general sales manager, Joe Frazer, suggested Plymouth as "a good old American name" the other executives balked. Frazer asked Chrysler, "Ever hear of Plymouth Binder Twine?" "Hell," replied Chrysler, "every goddam farmer in America's heard of that!" So Plymouth it was. *Jim Benjaminson, Robert Breckenridge*

placed by the Model U. It took a sharp eye to detect the differences between the two cars–most noticeable were the bumpers which remained two pieces but were now rounded, rather than flat, without the twin horizontal grooves found on the Q. Headlamps were changed from Depress Beam to Twolite, the hubcaps were larger, and the radiator nameplate read simply "Plymouth" rather than "Chrysler Plymouth." Tire size remained 4.75x20in, later replaced by 19in wheels. Wood wheels were standard with wires optional.

The biggest differences occurred underhood. The old Maxwell four had been completely revamped, moving the exhaust pipe from the rear of the engine to the front; the distributor drive housing was changed from a vertical to an angled position, front and rear main bearings were bigger, and the stroke increased 1/4in. Despite the changes, horsepower remained at forty-five. Additionally, prices were dropped for most body styles.

In April 1929 Plymouth celebrated its first "Thousand Car Day," building 1,002 vehicles. A seventh body style, a Deluxe sedan, was added. For his extra twenty dollars the Deluxe buyer got better upholstery and cowl lamps with bright trim cowl molding. Cars built after July 18, 1929, were considered to be 1930 models.

To meet the demand for the Plymouth, a new assembly plant was built in Detroit at the corner of Lynch Road and Mt. Elliott Avenue. Running 2,490ft long and containing 22.7acres of floor space under one roof and on one level, it was the largest automobile plant in the world. A second assembly plant, located across the Detroit River in Windsor, Ontario, supplied cars for the Canadian trade. Model Q production totaled 60,270 U.S. and 5,827 Canadian-built cars, Model U production raised those figures to 99,178 U.S. and 9,167 Canadian-built, pushing Plymouth to tenth place in the industry.

An "improved" Model 30U went into production April 5, 1930. With the exception of heavier

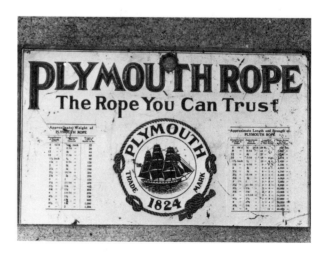

fenders, a prominent radiator shell, and an all-steel body, the 30U looked much like the Q and U models it replaced. The 30U was considered a 1930 model until car #1530345 was built on July l, then the 30U officially became a 1931 model. Despite March price cuts of sixty-five to seventy-five dollars per car and a fourteen-month production run, sales slipped to just 75,510 cars.

By now the nation's economy was in the strangle hold of the Great Depression. Realizing the position his dealers were in, Chrysler opened the Plymouth franchise to all his dealers (formerly Plymouth had been the exclusive property of Chrysler franchises), dualing Plymouth with Dodge and DeSoto dealers. The move served two purposes: the number of Plymouth dealerships swelled to over 7,000, and the low-priced Plymouth helped Dodge and DeSoto dealers stay alive when they found it impossible to sell their higher-priced cars. In its first year, one of every 100 cars sold had been a Plymouth. In its second year the ratio had risen to one in every fifty. Within another two years Plymouth would be the third best-selling car in the country, and by 1935 one of every four new cars sold would be a Plymouth.

The 30U proved to be a transitional model. Differences between early and late cars include a

The "Plymouth Parade" was a common dealer promotion to draw attention to the new car. The cars were shipped hidden beneath covers that had the letters of the car's name jumbled in the same manner as that displayed on the parade leader's uniform. *Chrysler Historical Foundation*

switch to oval rear windows (a Plymouth styling mark through the PA models), the addition of water and fuel pumps (replacing thermo-syphon cooling and a vacuum tank fuel supply), and the replacement of driveshaft leather "discs" with conventional universal joints.

The first Plymouth, sold to Ethel Miller of Turlock, California, was traded back to Chrysler when she took possession of the one millionth Plymouth in 1934. *Chrysler Historical Foundation*

The Model Q, here in roadster form, is easily identified by the flat, grooved bumper bars and radiator emblem reading "Chrysler-Plymouth." This car sports optional dual sidemounts and rare wire wheels. Owner: Loyd Groshong. *Jim Benjaminson*

The Model A touring car is a very rare, early Plymouth body style. Most touring cars were shipped overseas. Owner: Gene Fear.

The 30U engine's bore increased 1/4in with a subsequent increase from 45hp to 48hp. Bearings were again beefed up, and midway through production a switch was made to four rings per piston. Prices became more competitive, a 30U sedan costing $15 less than a comparable Model A and $50 less than a Chevrolet—while both of those marques continued to lose market, Plymouth climbed two more notches, to eighth place.

The 30U was replaced in May 1931 by the PA series, a car that would march Plymouth directly into the number three sales spot—a position it would occupy for the next twenty-five years. The "Big Two" had become the "Big Three." Walter Chrysler, legend has it, was so proud of the PA that he drove the third car off the line and headed across town to visit Henry and Edsel Ford in Dearborn. After showing the car to the Ford's, he presented them the keys and hailed a cab for home. (Chrysler Corporation's own history *Plymouth, Its First 40 Years* (and subsequent fiftieth anniversary edition), Langworth and Nordby's *Complete History of Chrysler Corporation*, and Nevin and Hill's *Ford: Expansion and Challenger: 1915-1933* all repeat this tale—but it may be more legend than fact.)

Corporate records show car number 1570303—the third PA Plymouth built—was shipped to Chicago. There are, of course, other possible explanations. The car, if the incident actually occurred, could have been a pre-production prototype, or it may have been the third car built on a particular day and not necessarily *the* third car ever built.)

Styling of the PA was more rounded, the oval rear window again serving as a Plymouth trademark. Radiators featured the first built-in grill and were capped by a highly detailed short-body "Flying Lady" cap. The four cylinder engine remained at 196ci but output rose from 48hp to 56hp. While the factory claimed 0–40mph in 9.7sec, the English magazine *The Motor* couldn't match those figures, taking 13sec just to reach 30mph, and 20sec to hit 40mph.

Again, it was under the hood where the greatest changes had taken place with Chrysler's introduction of "Floating Power." Called the "Fourth Milestone" in motoring by Walter Chrysler (the others included electric self-starting, enclosed bodies, and four-wheel hydraulic brakes), "Floating Power" was the work of Owen Skelton and the result of testing nearly 1,000 different mounts.

The 30U's prominent radiator shell differentiated it from earlier models. Later Plymouth roadsters used an oval rear window, whereas early cars had used a rectangular window. Owner: Floyd Carlstrom

The exceptionally rare PA phaeton—of 528 built just four are known to exist—was favored by President Franklin Roosevelt, who hept his at "The Little White House" in Warm Springs, Georgia. Owner: Dwight Cervin. *Ross McLean*

Lou Miller receives congratulations from K.T. Keller for his successful completion of the record setting coast-to-coast run. *Chrysler Historical Foundation*

PB's pour off the Lynch Road assembly line. Note the overhead sign advising drivers that "Free wheeling must be disconnected on all cars driven on factory premises." *Chrysler Historical Foundation*

Mounting the engine at three points—one point high (directly beneath the water pump), the other two points low (on the transmission housing)—the engine was suspended along its own center of gravity. Mounted in "sandwiches" of rubber, the engine could shake and vibrate but these vibrations were not transmitted to the frame or passenger compartment. Plymouth was also the only manufacturer among the low-priced three to offer free wheeling (free wheeling allowed shifting without clutching).

Louis B. Miller and co-drivers Earl Pribek and Russell Harding pulled a bone-stock PA sedan off the assembly line, fitted an auxiliary gas tank in place of the rear seat, and proceeded to set a transcontinental speed record from San Francisco to New York and back, covering the 6,287mi in 132hrs, 9min, at an average of 47.52mph.

PA production totaled more than 106,000 units including a stripped model called the PA Thrift and the upscale Deluxe sedan.

The last of the 4-cylinder Plymouths, the model PB went on line February 4, 1932, with ten body styles, including the largest line up of open cars ever offered by Plymouth. Unusual additions were a two door "Victoria" style convertible sedan and a long wheelbase 7-passenger sedan. Both would be one years offerings, although the 7-passenger would return to the lineup in 1934 and continue in production through 1941.

The PB was truly the zenith of the 4-cylinder cars, with styling that made it look like an expensive car. Borrowing touches from the custom car

Big news for 1933 was the 6-cylinder engine. Here engine blocks roll down the engine assembly line. *Chrysler Historical Foundation*

15

builders, the PB hood stretched from the radiator shell up over the cowl to the windshield posts. Free standing headlights, slanting windshields, and front opening "suicide" doors set the PB apart from the PA models.

The old four, with the same bore and stroke as the PA, was now pumping out 65hp thanks to larger valves, improved manifolds, and a change in the spark advance curve. The PB would be the shortest lived model (with the exception of the war-shortened 1942 models), the last car coming off the line September 27, 1932. Within days the huge Lynch Road plant was stripped to the bare walls—forty five days and 9 million dollars later it would be back on line, as production began on Plymouths first 6-cylinder cars. To bring the new PC series 6-cylinder cars to market, every machine tool in the building had been replaced.

The new car made its mark on automotive history by being introduced November 2, 1932, to the dealer network via the Columbia Broadcasting Company radio network. The brain child of Joe Frazer, the 1-1/2hr program went on the air at 1:00 p.m. narrated by popular commentator Lowell Thomas. The show featured Walter Chrysler, B. E. Hutchinson, Fred Zeder, and Harry G. Moock, along with race drivers Barney Oldfield and Billy Arnold. Daily newspapers the day prior to the broadcast read "Plymouth apologizes to the radio public for taking time on the air to tell 7,232 dealers about Walter P. Chrysler's new Plymouth." Coinciding with the broadcast were dealer meetings in twenty-five cities across the nation—each meeting coordinated by Western Union time clocks. At the appropriate time, the cars were unveiled simultaneously.

The biggest news, of course, was the new 6-cylinder engine. At 189ci, it had less displacement than the 4-cylinder it replaced but developed 70hp with standard 5.1:1 compression. An optional aluminum "Red Head" raised compression to 6.5:1 and horsepower to seventy-six. Free wheeling was continued with the addition of an automatic vacuum controlled clutch.

The new six was displayed under the ever-popular clear plastic hood—a gimmick Ford had used with its V-8 the year before and that Oldsmobile would repeat in 1949 for its overhead valve V-8. *Chrysler Historical Foundation*

Sales of the six soared–then plummeted. Much of the blame has been placed on the PC's poor styling; its broad, chrome-plated radiator shell, pancake headlamps, and short 107in wheelbase made it look more like a 4-cylinder automobile than the PB it replaced. Realizing a disaster in the making, a crash program was undertaken to bring out a bigger car for the spring selling season.

Pulling a longer wheelbase chassis from the DP series Dodge, the Plymouth's wheelbase was increased to 112in. While the body remained the same, longer front fenders, a longer hood, and a more upright painted radiator shell were fitted. A 1-1/4in dip in the front bumper and bullet-shaped stainless headlamps marked the differences between the PC and the new PD series. The PC was discontinued in April, being replaced by an upgraded model known as the PCXX which looked much like the PD with the exception of painted headlamps and straight-bar bumpers. For the first time in its history Plymouth offered the buyer two models.

These changes, along with an improving economy and government-mandated used car allowances (the NADA book went into effect November 30, 1933) saw Plymouth sales climb to an all time high of 261,088 cars.

Nineteen thirty-four introduced two series–the Deluxe PE and "New Plymouth Six" model PF, boasting an enlarged engine (201ci, 77hp) and independent coil spring front suspension. These were

First Lady Eleanor Roosevelt in her 1933 PD Convertible, taken July 4 at the White House. *Franklin Roosevelt Library*

This 1933 PD rumble seat coupe also sports dual sidemounts and external trumpet horns. The optional "Flying Lady" radiator cap has a longer, slimmer body than that used on the PA-PB. Owner: John Hogg.

This PE Deluxe two door sedan is fitted with optional Klaxon K-26 horns (same as used by 1932 Buicks) and twin windshield wipers. The PE differed from PF and PG models by having lou- vers and doors on the side of the hood. Some early PE's were shipped with wire wheels but most had steel artillery wheels as shown. Owner: Jim Benjaminson.

joined in March by the straight axle PG series "Standard Six." Offered only as a coupe and two-door sedan, the PG was aimed at the fleet market. April saw the addition of two special PE models, Plymouths first wood body station wagon (bodies built by U.S. Body & Forging) and the close coupled, blind quarter window Town Sedan with built-in trunk. The PF series was replaced mid year by

Open Plymouths never sold in great numbers—only 2.308 1935 PJ Deluxe ragtops were built. This car was restored by White Post Restorations for the late Jim Davis. *Westervelt*

Jimmie Lynch rigged an automatic-clutch-equipped Plymouth with a hood-mounted saddle and hidden controls and used this bucking steed to launch his long stunt-driving career. Lynch called his creation the "Mystery Horse Car." He later switched to Dodge, leading the Jimmie Lynch Death Dodgers stunt troop. *Texarkana Library*

the PFXX "Special Six," which differed chiefly in the addition of a glove compartment, an ash tray on the instrument board, and a chrome-plated windshield frame.

Sales continued to climb, surpassing the 1933 record. On August 8, 1934, another milestone was reached when the one millionth Plymouth, a PE four-door sedan, was driven off the line. Plymouth had accomplished in six short years what had taken Ford twelve years and Chevrolet nine years to achieve. The car was delivered to the Chrysler Pavilion at the Chicago World's Fair where it was ultimately delivered to Mrs. Ethel Miller of Turlock, California, who claimed to have purchased the first Plymouth sold in 1928. Final 1934 production came to 321,171 cars.

Nineteen thirty-five saw a switch to rounded styling, influenced no doubt by the Chrysler and DeSoto Airflows. Again, two models were offered, both coded the PJ series (a third PJ series built mostly in Canada was short lived). Unusual models for the year included two long wheelbase sedans, one, a long wheelbase five-passenger sedan with built–in trunk, the other a seven-passenger "flat-back" sedan with folding jumpseats. Oddly enough, the 1935 Plymouths returned to a straight-bar front axle. Engine improvements included full water jacketing and a vacuum controlled distributor. Sales surpassed 350,000 cars for the model year.

Fred Luther tries out the driver seat of the Plymouth-powered motorcycle. Skid plates on either side helped keep the bike upright and acted as brakes when needed. Steering was remotely controlled by chain and radiators above and below the engine helped keep it cool. *Chrysler Historical Foundation*

A painted center section in the grill and long, bullet-shaped painted headlamps were the most noticeable external changes for 1936. Sidemounted spare tires made their last appearance. Unusual options included a removable pickup box for the business coupe and a hearse/ambulance conversion for touring sedan models. Plymouth sales exceeded 500,000 units (520,025) for the first time in 1936.

Plymouth hit the market with an all new car for 1937—a true "fat fender" automobile, again offered in two model series called the "Business" and "Deluxe." Safety styling saw all dash knobs placed below the instrument panel, the windshield crank knob folded flush (this was the last year windshields opened for ventilation), door handles curved inward, and the back of the front seat heavily padded. A greatly improved economy saw sales soar to an all time high of 566,128 cars (excluding commercial vehicles), a record that would stand until 1950. Setting another record was sales of Deluxe models, chosen by 86.7 percent of purchasers, the highest such percentage ever in Plymouth sales history. The building of the two millionth Plymouth, a Deluxe Touring Sedan, also took place. Number two million also went to Mrs.

Ethel Miller of Turlock, California. Nineteen thirty-seven also marked Chrysler's recognition of the United Auto Workers Union following an eighteen day strike.

Plymouth rolled out its mildly restyled 1938 "Jubilee" models with high expectations for another banner sales year. Instead, the company was slapped in the face by a brief, severe recession. Sales throughout the auto industry slumped by nearly 50 percent. A shortened grill, bug-eye headlamps (which were repositioned mid-year), and a 12 percent price hike all helped keep buyers away from the showrooms. By years end, sales had dropped to 285,704 vehicles. Even a change in model names (the "Business" was now called the "Road King") didn't help.

For the Chrysler family, 1938 also proved to be a bad year. Walter was stricken with a circulatory ailment in May and was still convalescing when his beloved wife Della died of a cerebral hemorrhage on August 8. Walter had retired from active participation in Chrysler in 1935, though he would make a few more public appearances on its behalf.

A completely restyled Plymouth hit the showrooms early in September 1939—the first of any of

Station wagon popularity increased through the 1930s, though surviving examples are very rare today. This 1936 wagon, one of two known to exist, is built on the P1 Business chassis. Owner: Terry Dorrell.

A milestone for model year 1937 was the building of the one millionth car in a single year. On hand for the festivities are (L to R) "Pop" Sauerbray, Abraham van der Zee, unidentified, Joseph Field, unidentified, Dan S. Eddins, Walter P. Chrysler (in car), K.T. Keller, Fred Zeder, and B.E. Hutchinson. *Chrysler Historical Foundation*

Convertible production fell to its lowest level ever in 1938; just 1,900 were built. Owner: W. Ed Petersen. *Jim Benjaminson*

the new cars to make their appearance. With a deeply prowed front end and two-piece vee'd windshield, few people realized that the 1939s were built on the old 1937–38 body shells. Of the entire Chrysler lineup, Plymouth was the only to offer any open models, including a convertible coupe with the industry's first power-operated top and a four-door convertible sedan (the body was the same as used on the 1937–38 Chrysler and DeSoto convertible sedans).

Lower prices, an improved economy, and dashing good looks saw the 1939 models striving to recapture lost ground. Column shifting (on the Deluxe only) and a new "Safety Signal" speedometer that changed colors with the vehicle's speed helped Plymouth garner an Eastern Safety Conference Award.

Plymouth returned to independent front suspension for 1939, which would also be the last year for rumble seats.

As the first of the 1940 models rolled down the assembly line August 8, 1939, no one realized these new bodies would still be in production nearly ten years later. While there would be major chassis and engine changes with the 1942 model, the 1940 and succeeding 1941 would be the basis for the postwar models. Sales continued to grow, with one of every fourteen new cars sold being a Plymouth. Sales projections foresaw the possibility of Plymouth surpassing Ford as the nation's number two selling automobile (Chrysler Corporation as a whole had passed Ford some years earlier, making Chrysler the second largest auto company in the U.S.).

Only an all out effort by Ford with a new car for 1941 prevented Plymouth from attaining the number two spot. Unfortunately, in the near future Plymouth's market share would slowly begin to slip.

The 1941 Plymouth, offered in three distinct series known as the "Plymouth," "Deluxe," and "Special Deluxe," showed only minor improvements

True "Floating Power!" Stunt driver Lucky Teter leaps a semi-tractor in a ramp-to-ramp jump. Teter would be killed performing this stunt in 1942, driving the same 1938 Plymouth. *Jim Russell*

23

In 1939, the Deluxe convertible coupe was the only convertible offered in the entire Chrysler lineup. Heavy restyling hid the fact the body was the same as the 1937–38 convertible. *Chrysler Historical Foundation*

The 1939 convertible coupe was the first car in the industry to have a power-operated top. It was also the last convertible to have a rumble seat. *Chrysler Historical Foundation*

over the 1940, including a counter-balanced deck lid, alligator style hood opening, and underhood-mounted battery. Its most novel feature was the stop light mounted high on the center of the deck lid. Sales for 1941 climbed to 522,080, including delivery of two Quartermaster Corps fleet orders for military staff cars.

Nineteen forty-two models in Deluxe and Special Deluxe trim went into production in July 1941 with dealers and customers alike advised that "Plymouth automobile tools are rapidly being converted to tools for manufacturing of arms . . . hundreds of Plymouth workmen will be transferred to the factory's own war materials unit." Changes for 1942 included door panels flared at the bottom to cover the running boards and an odd "race car inspired" air scoop under the front bumper. A new model was the Town Sedan, which featured rear doors hinged at the front with quarter windows built into the door frame (regular sedans had suicide-style rear doors and quarter windows in the body). Underneath the body a perimeter box frame replaced the traditional X-member frame, while under the hood the old reliable 82hp 201ci six had been replaced by a 217ci 95hp engine pirated from sister division Dodge.

As America edged ever closer to all out war, "black out" models with painted–or missing–trim began making an appearance. Purchasers attempting to take delivery after January 1, 1942, found that all new cars in dealer inventories had been frozen by government edict; after January 10 only certain clientele–such as the military–or "critical" consumers such as doctors and nurses were allowed to purchase new cars. The last 1942 came off the line January 31, 1942. As the giant Lynch Road assembly plant converted for total war production, tools and dies for the 1942 models were moth balled. Some design work continued into the early months of 1943, working on what would have been 1943 and 1944 models. Other development work, such as the plastic-bodied car secreted around the streets of Detroit in 1942, was discontinued entirely.

Chrysler Corporation's World War Two production included 25,059 tanks; more than 500,000 Dodge army trucks; 93,339 Bofors guns; 3 billion ammunition rounds; 5,500 Sperry gyro compasses; 18,413 B29 bomber engines; 11,000 Curtis Hell

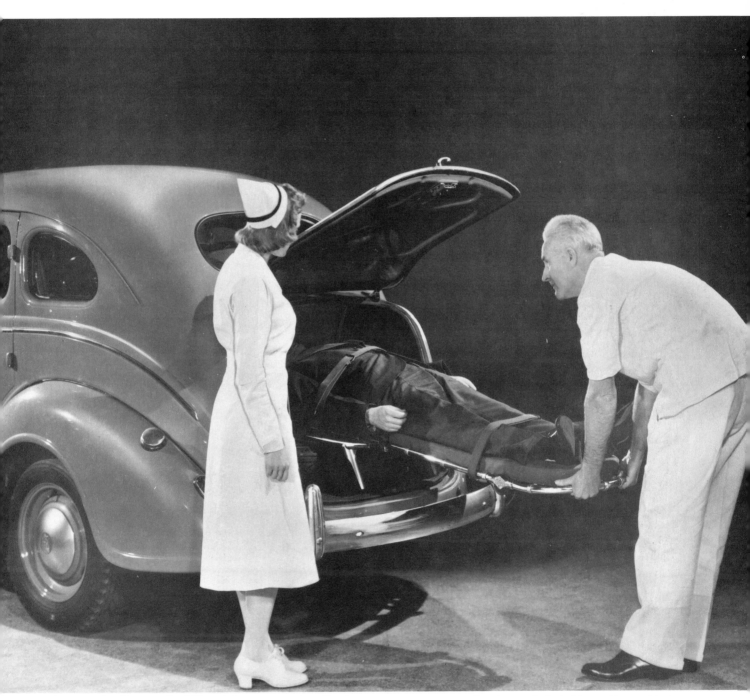

An unusual option was the $55 ambulance conversion offered on any Plymouth sedan. The partition between the trunk and the passenger compartment was eliminated to enable a cot to be inserted through the trunk. *Chrysler Historical Foundation*

The 1940 Deluxe two-door sedan sold new for $775—at least in advertising. Delivered price of this car was $1,020. Options included All Weather heating system with two heaters, pushbutton radio, and foglamps. Owner: Jim Benjaminson

The Safety Signal speedometer continued into 1940. The color appeared under the dot on the needle. The gauges all had a safety signal as well. Plastic control knobs are much sought after by restorers today. *Chrysler Historical Foundation*

This photo of a prototype 1941 sedan shows the full body molding used as the color break line for two-tone paint combinations. *Chrysler Historical Foundation*

Diver wings; 9,000 pontoons; 10,000 Corsair landing gears; and 5,000 B29 Bomber fuselages. Detroit, Michigan, had, in President Roosevelt's words, been turned into the "arsenal of democracy."

Despite the bleak years ahead—and perhaps to bolster the American spirit as the war raged on—magazines and periodicals regularly presented artists drawings of radically designed cars of the future. When a car-hungry nation caught its first glimpses of the actual postwar models no one really cared that they were simply "warmed over" pre-war models. There wasn't a factory in America that could build enough to keep up with demand!

The 1942 Town Sedan had a normal opening rear door and vent window built into the door frame. A one-year-only model, few were built. Owner: Bill Leonhardt

Actor Mickey Rooney had the honor of painting the numbers on the four millionth Plymouth built in 1941. Rooney, who starred in the "Hardy Boys" movie series, often drove the car in these films. *Chrysler Historical Foundation*

The last 1942 Plymouth built came off the line January 31, 1942. *Chrysler Historical Foundation*

"SHES BACK AMONG FRIENDS AGAIN"

THEY came smashing through the Jap lines and there it was — a 1941 Plymouth De Luxe Sedan in the heart of the New Guinea jungle!

On its side was painted the enemy's rising sun insignia. American bullets had drilled the machine so full of holes that the entire top had to be removed. But the motor, according to Staff Sgt. Kenneth B. Schooley, who described the incident, was "in excellent condition, despite having a few large-caliber bullets bounced off it."

After the usual rough jungle travel, he writes, "it's like riding on air." At last report, the sedan was no longer "De Luxe" but it was doing a real job on New Guinea. The medical detachment requisitioned it, took out the back seat, put in a floor, and was using the Plymouth to transport wounded troops from the front.

* * *

Plymouth records show that this historic car went from the factory to a dealer on Guam. Probably the Japs seized it there and took it with them to New Guinea. The full story won't be known until after the war – if then.

But there's no mystery about the reason why Plymouth is a great car on New Guinea or on Main Street. Plymouths were designed and manufactured to do their job under the worst conditions and the best. That quality is now going into Bofors anti-aircraft guns, assemblies for Helldivers, many other war needs. Meanwhile, three million Plymouths are proving their stamina on the roads. They may have to last a long time. They're built to do that when serviced by experienced Plymouth dealers.

PLYMOUTH Division of Chrysler Corporation

- TRUE YESTERDAY——

PLYMOUTH BUILDS GREAT CARS

- IN TRUST FOR TOMORROW

Plymouth continued to advertise during the war. This ad reads "She's Back Among Friends Again" and relates how American soldiers liberated a 1941 Deluxe sedan on New Guinea. "On its side was painted the enemy's rising sun insignia. American bullets had drilled the machine so full of holes that the entire top had to be removed. But the motor, according to Staff Sergeant Kenneth B. Schooley, who described the incident, was "in excellent condition, despite having a few large-caliber bullets bounced off it." A medical detachment requisitioned it, took out the back seat, installed a floor, and used it to transport wounded troops. Factory records showed the car had been shipped to Guam—how it had gotten to New Guinea was unknown. *Chrysler*

Chapter 2

1946–1948: An Incredible Seller's Market

As the war in Europe wound down, the U.S. government slowly began allowing the automobile industry to return to the business of making cars. It had been four years since any new cars had been built, and those cars still on the road were beginning to show their age. Driving had been curtailed during the war, but each motorist had been rationed a few gallons of gas per week, so the nation's automobile fleet was aging. According to *Fortune*, of the 29.6 million cars on the road at the start of World War II, only 22 million were still in use when the war ended, and half those cars were more than ten years old. Although the economy had grown in the immediate prewar years, there were still many people who had been unable to afford a new car then. "A majority of the hungriest prospects will not have 1942, 1941 or 1940 models to offer in trade but rather 1939s, 1938s and 1937s," wrote James Dalton, editor of *MoToR* magazine. Surveys taken showed a large percentage of the population intended to buy a new car when they again became available, some analysts predicting sales of 6 million vehicles per year for at least three years to catch up to the demand. "Car sales," Dalton wrote in the March 1946 issue, "were not likely to exceed 2.5 million unless existing materials shortages and other obstacles are eliminated much

sooner than now seems likely . . . Scarcity of steel, castings and textiles for body upholstery, will hold operations to 70 percent of prewar 'normals' even if no new difficulties develop." Dalton's predictions proved to be accurate as final 1946 calendar year sales came to only 2,149,000 cars, according to Automobile Manufacturers Association figures. The years 1947 and 1948 would be better (3.5 and 3.9 million cars, respectively), but shortages and strikes continued to keep the numbers down.

Chrysler Corporation was late in returning to the automobile business as it was committed to complete several government contracts, at the expense of civilian car production (Chrysler was the largest builder of tanks during not only World War II but Korea and Vietnam as well). Ford enjoyed an early start, partly due to a commitment made to it by the government. Ford Motor Company was floundering and on the verge of bankruptcy during the war, largely due to a lack of management. Henry Ford's active participation in the company was nil, the old man having suffered several strokes. His only son, Edsel, died early in 1943, leaving the company in the hands of a group of henchmen led by the ruthless Harry Bennett. In reality, the company was running on its own momentum. The U.S. government needed Ford's manufacturing facilities for the war effort so badly they pulled Henry Ford's grandson, Henry Ford II, out of the Navy and placed him in charge of the company. After the war, Ford received preferential treatment (as did Kaiser-Frazer) in receiving steel allotments to begin building automobiles once again. Of the total cars actually built in 1945, Ford Motor Company totals—Ford, Lincoln, and Mercury—accounted for 49.7 percent of industry production compared to GM's 33.5 percent. Chrysler Corporation's production was so minuscule that Nash moved up, if ever so briefly, to third place for 1945. Chrysler would not return to building automobiles until October. Plymouth production got off to an equally slow start, shipping just 684 Deluxe and 86 Special Deluxe cars in December. These 770 cars (not even half of one day's output before the war) were still

Marketplace(Calendar Year 1946)
  Chevrolet–18.3 percent
  Ford–17.3 percent
  Plymouth–11.3 percent
Marketplace(Calendar Year 1947)
  Chevrolet–19.7 percent
  Ford–16.8 percent
  Plymouth–9.8 percent
Marketplace(Calendar Year 1948)
  Chevrolet–19.8 percent
  Ford–14.0 percent
  Plymouth–9.7 percent

Fleet of the first postwar Plymouths leaves the Lynch Road factory. Note the wrapped bumpers and not a whitewall tire in sight. Only the second car from the left has the plastic whitewall insert. *Chrysler Historical Foundation*

Only Plymouth, Nash, and Lincoln continued to build convertibles without quarter windows after the war. The grille guard on this 1946 P15C is one of several types sold for these models. Owner: Don Knight *Jim Benjaminson*

Although two-door sedans were the most popular body style with Ford and Chevy buyers, Plymouth buyers preferred four-doors. Shown is a 1946 P15C Special Deluxe. Owner: Joe Abela.

good enough to rank Plymouth twelfth in sales. In 1945, 420 Dodges, 368 DeSotos, and 322 Chrysler Sixes brought Chrysler Corporation's total output to just 1,880 units. For Chrysler's 10,515 U.S. and 1,475 Canadian dealers, it would be an agonizing

A 4ft-diameter porcelain enamel DeSoto-Plymouth sign from the late 1940s. *Jim Benjaminson*

period waiting for new cars to arrive in their showrooms.

Before Plymouth could begin building new cars, the company faced the enormous task of converting the factories back to civilian use. The giant Lynch Road plant had been gutted of all auto making machinery, which had to be rebuilt and installed. Over 18,000 prewar machines were rebuilt, 20,000 machine tools set in place, over seventy miles of conveyors, 3,100 linear feet of spray booths, and one and a half miles of drying ovens reinstalled before production could begin.

Plymouth's new models for 1946 were once again offered in two series, the P15S Deluxe and P15C Special Deluxe. Deluxe body styles included a four-door sedan, two-door sedan, club coupe, and business coupe. Special Deluxes added a convertible coupe and wood-body station wagon to the lineup. Dealers were advised in January 1946, "Panel Delivery and Express Commercial Cars are not included in the Plymouth line at present," nor would they be at any time in the future. Pent-up demand and material shortages would see the P15 series built virtually without change until the early months of 1949. What cars had been built in 1945 were considered 1946 models; cars built after January 1, 1947, were considered 1947 models, as those built after January 1, 1948, were considered 1948s. Cars built after December 1, 1948, were considered 1949 models. These 1949 P15 models are also known as the "First Series" 1949s, being replaced by all new models in March.

Despite speculation as to what the new cars would look like, they did not, at first glance, appear much different than the 1942s. Wartime government restrictions on the auto companies had prohibited development work on new models. Some work was done, of course, but the only real improvements made during the war years came from technologies developed for the production of war goods. There was little time–or need–to design completely new automobiles after the war. Any car that could be built was sold as soon as it left the factory doors, regardless of who the manufacturer was.

In an effort to curb inflation, the government, through the Office of Price Administration, dictated the prices that could be charged for new cars. No restrictions were placed on used cars, and their prices soared. Even as late as 1948 as production levels began to catch up with demand, prices of used cars were frequently higher than the advertised prices of new cars. The author's father pur-

chased a one-owner 1940 Plymouth Deluxe two door in August 1948, paying $1,050 for it ($30 more than the original owner paid in 1940!). List price for a 1948 Special Deluxe two door was $1,392.

Waiting lists were common at dealerships. Those wanting a new car placed their name–and often a cash deposit–with the dealer. Customers hoped that as new cars became available, they would move up the list until it was their turn to take delivery. Car buyers with their name on every dealer's list in town were not uncommon; reports of money paid under the table were common, as were scalpers who would put their new car on the market at a price considerably higher than they had paid for it. Because the dealer's price was regulated by the government, many dealers loaded the cars up with every accessory possible to increase the profitability of the unit. W.B. Rice, Plymouth's director of service, realized the seller's market wouldn't last forever. In a letter to dealers in June 1947, he wrote, "Barring the atomic bomb, flying saucers, and international complications, we'll soon find ourselves in a buyer's market." Rice's prediction for the future did come true, but during the lifetime of the P15 models it remained very much a

Postwar sales of Plymouth's converted to DeSoto's soared following WWII. Sold new in Mexico, this DeSoto Diplomat (coded model SP15) had a metric speedometer and a temperature gauge marked in Celsius. *Carlos Heligman*

The business coupe used a different body than the club coupe as can be seen by the small quarter window. Owner: Pete Fischer.

Rear view of the P15 wagon shows the intricate wood work. The factory recommended refinishing the wood every six months—or more often if needed. Owner: David L. Kotsch.

seller's market. To capitalize on the seller's market, Plymouth began advertising the new cars before the first one had even been built—the first ad appearing in the September 6, 1946, issue of *U.S. News*.

The first post-war Plymouth, a P15S Deluxe, came off the line October 22, 1945. Special Deluxes would follow four days later. Bodies for the P15 Plymouths were virtually unchanged from 1942, with only minor trim differences. Plymouth literature claimed fifty improvements over the prewar cars—many were of little significance but were changes nonetheless. In profile, the cars looked much the same. It took a frontal view to see the differences in the new cars. The grille followed the same design motif used since 1939, only now the bars were no longer divided across the front of the car; they fell in an alternating wide and narrow pattern. The oblong parking lamps were moved to a spot directly below the headlights and were incorporated into the ends of the third wide bar. A new ship emblem, set in a heavy chrome molding (and no longer enamel) was attached to the lower end of the hood. The word "Plymouth" was mounted in stainless block letters between this emblem and the top grille bar. The hood ornament was changed but

still employed a plastic insert with the ship outline molded into the plastic. The front bumper now wrapped around the fender to the wheel opening—two bumper overriders were standard on all Special Deluxes and optional (until April 7, 1947, when they became standard) on Deluxes. Adding to the clean looks of the car was the omission of the "air scoop" under the front bumper.

All side trim including front fender, body side, and rocker panel moldings were wider and smoother, eliminating the grooved trim used in 1942. The front fender molding was shorter than before, and the rear fender molding was eliminated entirely. There were cars fitted with rear fender moldings, but these were aftermarket items, or Dodge/DeSoto rear fender moldings added by the dealers. The rear fenders had a smaller wheel opening cutout than before, though the fender shape was unchanged (and could be interchanged with the 1942).

None of the closed cars used window reveal moldings as used on the 1942 Special Deluxe; the P15 Special Deluxe used a bright metal windshield surround and center divider bar, and Deluxe cars used a rubber surround and painted divider. At the

After sidemounts were discontinued, Plymouth struggled with where to mount the spare tire. Eventually it settled for this recess behind the driver's seat, cramping the left rear passenger's leg room. The second and third set of seats could be removed (and were interchangeable) for more carrying capacity. *David Kotsch*

Rear fender stone guards were optional on this 1947 P15C sedan. True to Plymouth tradition, four-door sedans outsold all other body styles. Owner: Albert Sywassink.

rear the only changes were in the stop and tail-lamps. The central stop light was enlarged and raised higher on the deck lid. A separate ship emblem was eliminated, being molded instead into the

Plymouth convertibles from 1932 to 1948 shared the same 6x24in rear window which restricted rear vision. Weather permitting, the rear curtain containing the metal-framed window would be zipped open. Owner: Ron Woolsey.

glass of the stop light lens. The taillamps protruded slightly more, with die-cast bezels rather than stainless steel. The license plate bracket was separate and no longer mounted on the base of the stop light molding. Again, most cars were fitted with two bumper overriders.

Mechanically there were few changes. The 217ci engine was still rated at 95hp, attained at 3600rpm instead of 3400rpm. The compression ratio was reduced from 6.8:1 to 6.6:1 (export cars had compression of 5.6:1 due to poor gas quality abroad in the postwar period). An economy engine package using a smaller intake manifold and carburetor with 1in bore returned to the option list. Rear-end ratio on cars equipped with this engine was 3.73:1. Manifold heat shields and a hardened steel throttle stop could also be added to the economy package. Aluminum pistons replaced the cast iron ones that had been mandated during the war. Like many vendors, Carter couldn't supply enough of their model D6G1 carburetors to meet Plymouth's production demands. Stromberg, which normally supplied Ford, provided its model 3-84 carburetor; the Stromberg carb required a different fuel line as it fed on the right side rather than from the front like the Carter. During this period, Carter substituted its model 574-S, a small bore carburetor with 1-

1/4in diameter, in place of the normal 1-1/2in throat. Cars built up to November 1946 used "cross and roller" universal joints at the rear of the propeller shaft in place of Chrysler's usual "ball and trunnion" type. When ball and trunnion u-joints were again available (with Special Deluxe car number 11603698 and Deluxe number 15189401) they were again used. Replacing the disposable oil filter was a new cleanable canister that contained a replacement cartridge. A heavy-duty (removable cartridge) filter was available as a dealer-installed kit. Engine dust pans marched into history October 15, 1946. In the early days they had been a selling point with the promise of keeping the engine compartment clean. Their elimination was claimed to provide better underhood cooling.

Plymouth's normal clutch plate supplier, Borg & Beck, was unable to satisfy demand so some cars used Auburn clutches instead. "Power Matic" shifting was no longer cataloged as a regular accessory though it could be special ordered, along with such driving aides as a vacuum clutch for disabled veterans. Vendor strikes plagued the industry, forcing changes in specifications and equipment. Engines

built during October 1948 had to be fitted with steel camshafts rather than the normal cast iron shafts. Hardened steel oil-pump drive-gears were necessary with the steel camshaft. When the steel camshaft was replaced the valve tappets did not have to be replaced, but if the tappets were replaced, the camshaft also had to be replaced, along with the oil-pump drive-gear. Cars fitted with the steel camshafts had the letter "S" following the engine serial number. Another unseen change came in December 1948 when a narrow ring gear replaced the old wide-style gear. The new gear could be used on old flywheels, but the older ring gear would not fit on the new flywheel.

A change appreciated by most drivers was the switch from the foot-operated starter pedal to a push button on the dashboard. Previously, stepping on the starter pedal had manually engaged the starter gear with the flywheel, at the same time engaging the switch to start it turning. The dash-mounted button activated a solenoid, which in turn engaged the starter. For the first time since 1928 there was no provision made to manually hand crank the engine. The coil was moved from its fa-

This 1947 P15C club coupe sports whitewall tires, a common dress up item on postwar cars today. Whitewall tires were unavailable from the factory in 1947. Owner: Carol Kastler.

Fulton sunvisors were popular aftermarket accessories for the P15 series Plymouths. In later years, Plymouth would begin marketing their own MoPar sunvisor. Owner: Terry Summers.

miliar firewall location to a position on top of the spark plug wire loom, shortening the coil wire considerably.

Cars built up to August 1946 used the same coil springs as in 1942, until Special Deluxe 11507116 and Deluxe 15157509, when the left front spring was changed to compensate for the weight of the car with a driver on board. These new front springs, rated at an extra 65lb load carrying capacity, carried the same part number as the right front spring. Identification between the two springs was by five hash marks on left springs and four hash marks on the right. At this same point a switch was made from synthetic BUNA rubber tubes to synthetic BUTYL rubber. The BUTYL tubes could be identified by a 3/8in blue stripe around its circumference. Two months later, the link-type sway bar, used since 1942, was replaced by a solid bar, effective with Special Deluxe 11513634 and Deluxe 15158443. All eight rear spring leaves were tapered on Special Deluxe cars, with only the second and third leaf (of seven) tapered on Deluxe models.

Standard tire size was 6.00x16in on all body styles. The diamond pattern tread used on rear tires prior to the war was discontinued, replaced by a rib tread used on all four tires. If a car was to be fitted with 6.50x16in tire, it was mandatory that 4-1/2in wide rims be used in place of the standard 4in rims. The only noticeable change in the P15 Plymouths came late in November 1947. Beginning with Detroit-built Special Deluxe 11851594 and Deluxe

U.S. Body & Forging continued to build wooden bodies for Plymouth station wagons after the war. Owner: Mark Sanny. *Jim Benjaminson*

The club coupe had a longer roof to accommodate back-seat passengers. Owner: Bill Robertson.

Taken when new in 1948, this Special Deluxe had whitewall inserts and the ever-popular Fulton sunshade. Plymouth would later offer its own sun visor as an add-on accessory. *Ned Booher*

15251917, the factory began switching to 15in wheels and Goodyear Super Cushion 6.70x15in tires. Los Angeles- and Evansville-built cars didn't make the switch until December, Los Angeles with Special Deluxe 25036148 and Deluxe 26010991, and Evansville with Special Deluxe 20234249 and Deluxe 22063548. Several tire manufacturers began offering a 6.70x16in tire about this same time, a tire Plymouth engineers found acceptable for all models except the station wagon. Government regulations dictated that spare tires and tubes could not be shipped with cars, including dealer drive-aways, a regulation that was lifted in December 1946. New car prices were adjusted accordingly when the spare again became standard equipment.

Restrictions also made whitewall tires unavailable, so all cars built from July 1946 on were equipped with either white plastic wheel covers to simulate the look of a whitewall, or stainless steel wheel rings. These wheel covers fit under the regular hubcap and covered all of the wheel–the "whitewall" rings had a black stripe next to the hubcap itself. Effective September 8, 1947, all cars equipped with plastic wheel covers had the wheels painted one solid color instead of body color with paint striping, as had been done previously. These wheels were painted in Ecosheen (gray) enamel on Detroit- and Evansville-built cars, and black on Los Angeles-built cars. Wheels on cars equipped with stainless steel trim rings would still be painted body color and striped.

Interior changes were minimal. A new pattern of wood graining was used on the dash and garnish moldings in a lighter shade than in 1942. The Safety Signal speedometer colors were more intense and both the speedometer and gauges used an almost black background. The top molding of the dash was smooth, rather than ribbed, and curved around the ends to meet the lower molding, which

was still ribbed. The areas to the left of the speedometer and the glovebox door were painted brown. The panel to the left of the speedometer held the starter switch button.

A plate was added above the radio grille on Special Deluxe models, using the same brown color flanked by two chrome end caps. The word Plymouth appeared in the brown center section. The ship emblem was removed from the top half of the radio grille and a round plastic emblem was used on the lower half of the grille bearing the words "Special Deluxe." Deluxe models did not come with a radio grille unless a radio was installed, in which case the grille had to be installed as well. All control knobs remained in the same position as 1942 and were finished in oyster white. The knobs were now wedge shaped rather than concave. Exterior and interior door handles and window handles were the same as 1942. Escutcheons for the handles were of a slightly different pattern. Steering wheels were also brown to match the dash color; the finger grips used in 1941 and 1942 were eliminated. Special Deluxe cars had a full-circle horn ring with "Plymouth" and the Mayflower sailing ship in the middle.

The same two basic upholstery patterns used in 1942 were continued, with slight variations. One was a pin-striped broadcloth and the other a pile fabric. Broadcloth seems to have been used more than the pile. Each came in blue-gray or gray-green colors, the upholstery color generally matching the exterior paint color. Deluxe models had only one pattern, which differed from the Special Deluxe cars. Door panels on early models used the same material in the lower portion of the door as the seats, with a harmonizing solid color in the top part separated by a sweeping bright molding. Later models used a solid color on the panel. The lower portion of the seats, as well as the doors, utilized a red simulated-leather scuff panel. Deluxe buyers had to settle for a manually controlled dome lamp (it was automatic on Special Deluxes) and do without a glovebox lock, horn ring, front door armrests, door checks, assist straps, coat hooks, simulated rear floor carpeting, rear ash tray, and fixed quarter windows. A single windshield wiper was standard on the Deluxe line, but all cars were factory-equipped with two wipers, unless the buyer specifically asked for it to be deleted.

Rear seat robe cords on four-door sedans were eliminated in 1946 as the supply on hand ran out, and in June 1948 "Airfoam" seat cushions were installed on all Special Deluxe business coupes, club coupes, and two- and four-door sedans. The airfoam cushion was factory installed at an additional charge to the buyer of $7.50 for front seats only and $15 if installed on the rear cushion as well. Airfoam cushions were not available on the Deluxe. Special Deluxe buyers could have them deleted on special order. The lack of heater fan motors found cars fitted with the optional, dual heater MoPar All Weather Aircontrol System equipped with just one

motor, in the right hand unit. Heaters shipped after July 1947 were supplied with both motors, with a service package released in September to retrofit heater motors already in the field. The service package was treated as an option and not as a recall.

U.S. Body & Forging continued to supply Plymouth with wood-bodied station wagons as it had since 1934. Buyers still had a choice of light maple or mahogany side panels (first offered in 1942). Seat upholstery was now leatherette, with real leather an extra cost option. All wagons came with three seats, the rear two removable and interchangeable. The spare tire was carried in a special holder built into the rear of the driver's seatback, severely cramping the legroom of the passenger directly behind the driver. Standard station wagon color was Cruiser Maroon, with Battalion Beige optional. Plymouth's other colors "may be ordered for shipments later," according to a factory bulletin. Two-tone paint jobs on regular models, which had been optional in both 1941 and 1942, were no longer offered.

The convertible coupe was one of the last American-made cars to have a "Victoria"-style top without a rear quarter window (the other two were Nash and Lincoln). It was also the last Plymouth convertible to use vacuum cylinders to raise or

The convertible listed for $1,186 when introduced in 1946. By August 1948, the price had risen to $1,758. More than 15,000 were sold. This 1948 model is identified by its 15in wheels.. Owner: Robert Black.

lower the top. The control switch for the top was mounted on the far right side of the dashboard, presumably so the driver couldn't operate the top while the car was in motion. Standard top color was black with light gray optional at no extra cost.

Plymouth continued to be a popular supplier of taxi cabs, offering two packages to the trade. Package one, which retailed at $25, included commercial duty springs front and rear, special firm-ride shock absorbers, an 11in clutch plate and one-half gauge heavier seat cushion springs. Package two, at $15, included everything in the previous package with a 10in clutch plate. Leather upholstery, which had long been offered as an option on all models, was now a $70 option aimed specifically at the taxi market, available only on four door sedans.

During the P15's lifetime only one other noticeable exterior change was made, but you had to be sharp eyed to notice it. The door lock cover was changed in mid-1946, from the smooth Hurd-style used in years past to a spring-loaded (and heavier) cover shaped somewhat like a bell.

More than one million P15s were manufactured between October 22, 1945, and January 28, 1949, when the last car was built. Shipments of P15s in stock continued through March, the January shipment of 35,586 Special Deluxe cars (along with 5,676 Deluxes) setting the sixth highest single month's shipment in the P15's history. February's shipment dwindled to 1,445 Special Deluxe and 307 Deluxe cars, with the last 15 cars (all Special Deluxes) shipped in March. Plymouth's market share had eroded slightly each year since 1940 but not enough to nudge Plymouth from its traditional third place. Prices, despite government controls, had continued to escalate to the point where the price asked for the most expensive P15 in March 1946 would not buy the least expensive model in August 1948. Despite price hikes, steel shortages, and labor strikes it still remained very much a seller's market.

The Special Deluxe instrument panel had a radio grille whether the car had a radio or not. *Chrysler Historical Foundation*

Deluxe instrument panel was rather spartan, but when equipped
with a radio it got Special Deluxe trim. *Chrysler Historical Foun-*
dation

Chapter 3

1949–1954: Bigger on the Inside, Smaller on the Outside

1949: A New Car at Last

Plymouth was the last of the "Big Three" to unveil its "true" 1949 models. Ford had been the first, with a debut early in 1948, followed by Chevrolet. All three cars were revolutionary in design, at least compared to their 1946–48 counterparts. Ford's new "shoe box" concealed a host of mechanical improvements, including independent front coil spring and rear leaf suspensions, while Chevrolet's "stove bolt" six remained basically unchanged. Chevrolet bodies were styled in two categories, the now popular shoe box, and the familiar fastback .

Chrysler Corporation entered its silver anniversary year with a $90 million investment in bringing its 1949 line up to market. True to its heritage, the all-new Plymouth was conservatively styled (in what would later become known as the "Keller [for Chrysler President K.T. Keller] three-box school of

The most popular car in the line was the P18 Special Deluxe four-door sedan. Ribbed bumpers gave the car an expensive look, and proved quite popular with customizers. Owner: Paul Taylor

styling"–one box piled on top of two boxes laid end to end). The new cars rode a longer wheelbase yet were 4-3/16in shorter overall than the P15 they replaced. This "larger on the inside, smaller on the outside" concept was again blamed on Chrysler's president. "The American motorist is tired of having his hat knocked off every time he gets in or out of a car," wrote Wayne Whittaker in the April 1949 issue of *Popular Mechanics*, before quoting Keller directly: "As far as design goes we wanted to build an outstanding car, a car that is easy to get into and get out of, that is easy to garage, to handle in traffic or when parking. The outsides of our new cars are actually sculptured around conditions prescribed for the inside." When it came to automobile design Keller was conservative to a fault. "A car shouldn't knock your hat off–or your eyes out either," he is quoted as saying, nor should the hood be so low "you can piss over it." The 1949 Plymouth was truly a car K.T. Keller could love.

The first of the all-new second series 1949 Plymouths, a Special Deluxe, was completed on New Year's Eve, 1948. Long wheelbase Deluxe models followed on January 14 with the short wheelbase Deluxe not going on line until March 7, 1949. To help meet demand for the new cars a second California assembly plant went on-line in May at San Leandro.

The Mayflower ornament continued to lead the way down the nation's highways. *Jim Benjaminson*

The 1949 was offered in three series on two different wheelbases. At the bottom of the ladder was the P17 Deluxe. Built on a 111in wheelbase, it was the most austere in terms of trim, bright work, and upholstery. The P17 came in three body styles, a cozy single seat, three-passenger businessman's coupe, a five-passenger fastback two-door sedan, and the revolutionary new two-door all-steel-body Suburban station wagon.

The P18 Deluxe was built on the longer 118-1/2in wheelbase, and like the P17 Deluxe, was devoid of much external bright work, but featured slightly better interior appointments. The P18 Deluxe was built in two body styles, a two-door notchback club coupe and four-door sedan. (Why Plymouth decided to have two models with two different wheelbases designated "Deluxe" has never been explained. If chronological order were followed, at least one of these cars should have been the P16. Perhaps this engineering code was reserved for the Cadet, a 105-1/2in wheelbase economy car Plymouth was developing at the time. The Cadet reached full mockup stage in 1947 and could have been ready for the 1949 model year, but the project was canceled.)

The P18 Special Deluxe on the same 118-1/2in wheelbase enjoyed more external bright work and considerably more luxurious interiors. Special Deluxe models included a club coupe, four-door sedan, convertible club coupe, and a wood body four-door station wagon, which now had a steel roof and steel lower tailgate. For the first time all models, except the P17 two door, had external door locks on both front doors.

From the cowl forward, all three series shared the same sheet metal, grille, and bumper. Four-door sedan doors were now hinged at the front, and for the first time since 1942, rear quarter windows were placed in the door frames rather than the body. The second series 1949 Plymouth was all new–not a single piece of sheet metal, glass, or trim was retained from previous years. The headlamps, mounted nearly 1-1/2in higher and 4in farther apart, used the new bull's-eye sealed beams. The grille was wider but still recognizable in terms of the P15 grille work. Individual letters spelling out "Plymouth" were mounted on the hood, just above a trim piece on the hood's leading edge. A seam molding running the length of the hood was only partially covered by a redesigned and all-metal Mayflower sailing ship. Three wide and two narrow grille bars alternated down the face of the car, with the parking lamps set under the headlamps and surrounded by the edges of the widest middle and lower grille bar. The front bumper was unique as it, too, had three horizontal ribs, giving the car a delicate, yet expensive look. (These bumpers, like the ribbed bumpers of the 1937 DeSoto, would prove to be popular with the hot rod and custom car set.)

The most beautiful instrument panel in a low-price car was found in the 1949 Plymouth. *Jim Benjaminson*

Among the least expensive models was the P17 Deluxe 111in wheelbase three-passenger coupe. With a huge trunk and a short passenger compartment, these cars seemed out of place even when new but have proven to be extremely popular among today's collector. Owner: Ward Duffield.

The hood and deck lid were much lower, but still sat several inches above the fenders. A heavy belt molding separated the more rectangular "greenhouse" from the lower body, and a larger windshield (37 percent more area but still of the two-piece, flat glass variety) and larger rear window with "blind" rear quarters contributed to the car's formal flavor.

Front fenders blended neatly into the front doors, but attempts at blending the rear fenders into the body were not as successful as Plymouth still retained detachable rear fenders. These fenders were one of Plymouth's selling points and from a repairman's point of view were easier to replace than the non-detachable fenders used on either a Ford or Chevrolet.

The taillamps sat high atop the rear fender and formed a slight "fin" in their housing, which helped conceal the fender-to-body seam. For the first time, the taillamp lenses were plastic. The separate brake light was centrally located on the deck lid, just above the trunk handle and below the license plate. An indentation in the deck lid was provided for the license plate and bracket with a heavy medallion containing the word "Plymouth" and an enameled (Special Deluxe only) Plymouth crest mounted directly above the plate. As in the front, the attractive three-ribbed wrap-around bumper contributed to the elegant look of the new car.

Body side moldings on all models included a spear running from the headlamps to the trailing edge of the front fender and a second spear on the rear fender. Special Deluxe models had a chrome gravel shield on the leading edge of the rear fenders as well. (Various pieces of sales literature alternately show Deluxe models with and without this trim.)

Despite all the horizontal visual "cues" designed into the car, it still had a rather high, boxy appearance and sat too high off the ground. This problem was cured early in production by shortening the front coils and flattening the rear springs, to achieve a 1in drop in front and 1-1/2in drop in the rear.

All models were treated to one of the most stunning instrument panels ever placed in a low-priced automobile. On the rich, dark wood-grained panel, directly in front of the driver were three circular white-on-black dials; in the middle of the panel a chrome radio grille and mesh cascaded down to a heavy chrome molding running along the bottom of the panel from door to door. Set into the molding were the new key-start ignition switch, rotary light switches and other knobs, and the ash tray. To the right of the radio grille was a panel containing a ship ornament, which could be replaced by an electric clock. Optional heater systems, although an "add-on" accessory, were designed to blend into the design, mounting the controls directly beneath the radio. An unseen change was the switch to a magnetic fuel gauge in place of the bi-metal strip used in years past.

Window mechanisms were redesigned to permit full up-and-down travel in one and a half turns of the window handle, a feature that didn't receive much advertising. Trivial as it may sound, the highly-geared windows meant the driver didn't have to take his hands from the wheel as long to roll down the window as on other cars. Front seat cushions were increased 5in and rear cushions 6in in width, with legroom in the rear seat increased to 42-1/2in. Advertised as "chair height," the seats could have extra springs added to firm them up; Airfoam seat cushions were optional on all models except the P17 two door, Suburban, and woody station wagon.

Mechanical changes in the second series 1949s were modest at best. The frame was still the box perimeter type with four cross members as used since 1942. Steering ratio was unchanged at 18.2:1. Front wheel brakes continued to use the upper and lower wheel cylinders introduced on the P15 models. Engine displacement was unchanged at 217ci, with horsepower up to ninety-seven. This change came about through a newly designed cylinder head that raised compression from 6.7:1 to 7.0:1. A new intake manifold provided better distribution of the fuel-air mixture, fuel pump capacity was increased, and a fully automatic electric choke prevented "over" choking. New oil control rings with wider drainage slots and a chrome-plated top piston ring, along with improved crankcase ventilation, were also claimed. A larger starter motor, resistor spark plugs and weather-proofed ignition system aided in cold and wet weather starting. A welcome change in the electrical system replaced fuses with a circuit breaker system. Rear axle ratio on P17 models was 3.73 and 3.9 on all P18s. Rear axles in all models were of the semi-floating, hypoid design with ratios of 3.54, 4.1, and 4.3 optional at no additional cost. Gas tank capacity remained at 17gal, with an Oilite fuel filter mounted in the tank.

The least expensive car in the Plymouth lineup was the P17 business coupe. Designed for the businessman, the cozy little three-passenger car offered nearly unlimited carrying capacity. Surprisingly, the fastback two-door sedan proved to be the best seller in the P17 series. The landmark offering had to be the new all-steel two-door Suburban. With the rear seat in place there was 42in of cargo space available; with the seat folded down, another 26-1/2in was added. In a departure from the other wagons, the Suburban carried its spare tire in a well under the rear floor. While the P17 line was intended to be an economy series, the Suburban, at $1,840 was exceeded in price only by the convertible and four-door woody station wagon!

The value of the all-steel wagon was not lost on Plymouth buyers and 19,220 were sold, accounting for 3.7 percent of all 1949 Plymouths sold. Compared to the 3,443 four-door wagons sold, it was obvious Plymouth had a winner on its hands. There was only one year (1941) when station wagons accounted for more than 1 percent of production. In future years, sales of wagons would continue to grow—5.6 percent in 1950 and 9.75 percent in 1954—until 1958 when the station wagon would be the largest selling body style in the Plymouth lineup. Years later the 1958 *Dell's Car Buyers Guide* would call the Suburban "probably the most functional automobile built after the Model T."

The Suburban did have as standard equipment some items not found on the other P17s, such as two sun visors, dual horns, front bumper guards,

Often criticized as the "Keller three-box school of styling," even the sporty convertible looked short and stubby, despite riding on a 118-1/2in wheelbase. Owner: Harold Bailey. *Jim Benjaminson*

rear-seat armrests, dome light, and nine-leaf rear springs (seven leaves were standard on the coupe and two door, eight leaves on Special Deluxes). Standard tire size on all P17s was 6.40x15in Goodyear Super Cushions (6.70x15in on the long wheelbase cars, mounted on 4-1/2in rims); 18in wheels were optional on the Suburban only. An oil filter was extra, the rear springs were uncovered, and no crankshaft vibration dampener was furnished.

Standard upholstery in the business coupe was woven fiber fabric with dark red vinyl resin fabric door panels. This same material could be ordered for seat cushions and backs at no charge, with striped broadcloth available at extra cost. Standard upholstery in the two door was striped broadcloth, with no other options. Suburban buyers had the choice of light tan or dark tan vinyl resin seats and seatbacks and woven fiber headlining.

The P18 Deluxe was intended as a fleet sales unit. The P18 Special Deluxe, which cost about $80 more, easily outsold the P18 Deluxe by a four-to-one margin. It differed from the Special Deluxe in not having bright trim around the windshield and rear window and by the lack of a radio grille (which had to be purchased and installed if a radio was ordered). Checkered broadcloth was the only upholstery offered. Door armrests, glovebox lock, and horn ring were options.

Special Deluxe models were easily recognizable at a distance by the bright trim around the windshield and rear window, as well as the stainless stone guards on the leading edge of the rear fenders. Interiors were upgraded accordingly, with a choice of green or blue broadcloth, or green or blue pile fabric depending on the outer body color. Upholstery in the convertible club coupe was Bedford Cord with bolsters in red, blue, or green vinyl, again depending on car color. In addition to the regular colors, convertibles could be ordered in two special colors, Mexico Red or Plymouth Cream.

Electric motors replaced the vacuum cylinders on the convertible's power-operated top, and for the first time, convertibles were fitted with quarter windows. Convertible owners welcomed the clear plastic rear window, which had more than doubled in size from previous years.

The eight-passenger woody station wagon was upholstered in tan vinyl with exterior colors limited to Malibu Brown, Edmonton Beige, or Rio Maroon. The big wagon had removable center and rear seats, whereas the Suburban rear seat simply folded over. The center seat in the woody wagon could also be folded forward to aide entry to the rear-most seat. Where to carry the spare tire was finally resolved when a semi-recessed receptacle was built into the lower portion of the tailgate. Covered by a circular, rearward-swinging access door, the tire was neatly hidden from view. The little "bustle"

Almost always incorrectly referred to as a "two-door," this model is correctly known as the "club coupe," here seen in P18 Deluxe trim. Owner: Tom Martenson.

gave the car a "continental" look in addition to providing the rear-seat passenger with more legroom. A special rear bumper had to be employed on the wagon, with the center section hinged to swing down out of the way when the spare was removed or when the lower tailgate was opened. This arrangement also allowed rear bumper overriders, the first Plymouth wagon so equipped.

Typically considered an under-powered car, the 1949 Plymouth actually held its own against the competition. Chevrolet claimed only 90hp, with the Ford V-8 claiming 100hp (just five more than its 6-cylinder cars). Despite its turtle-slow reputation, Plymouth found its way to the winners' circle on many occasions. Stock car racing in those days was exactly that—the cars were not modified in any form. Except for taping the headlights, removing the hubcaps and muffler, and tying down the hood, the cars were as they came off the showroom floor. One of the first to see the winners' circle from behind the wheel of a Plymouth was a Level Cross, North Carolina tobacco farmer by the name of Lee Petty. Having wrecked the family Buick in a race at Charlotte, Petty reasoned the little 1949 Plymouth business coupe at the local dealership would be easier on tires and gasoline than the bigger cars. Petty's hunch proved to be right as he coasted to a first-place finish in his next race. Nicknamed "The Rock, one seventh and two second-place finishes were enough to put Petty and Plymouth in second place in the season's final points championship. When asked how he did it, Petty explained in a 1954 interview, "I could go through the turns flat out and when an Olds was trying to dig off the curve, I had a running start on him. I ran a 4.78:1 rear axle, lower than any of the other boys were using. And that little motor was doing full revs all the time. I found that Chrysler Imperial springs, shocks, wheels, etc., fit perfect beneath a Plymouth.

Still built by U.S. Body & Forging, 1950 would mark the last year for Plymouth's wood body station wagon. Owner: Ernest Fodor.

That made it handle fine, and the changes were legal. The Plymouth wouldn't do but 92mph wide open, but I tuned it so the car ran top speed lap after lap. The other boys blew tires or ran hot. Then

Fulton sun visors continued to be popular accessories, so much so that Plymouth began making their own visor for parts-counter sales. *Jim Benjaminson*

I moved in." Petty managed to put the little Plymouth among the first three cars in nineteen consecutive races to the chagrin of other drivers who charged he was running a souped-up motor. The engine was torn down fifteen times during that nineteen-race stretch and found to be bone stock each time.

Petty's victories were not flukes as Plymouths across the country began to score more wins. On October 16, 1949, another Plymouth, driven by Walt Faulkner, scored a first-place victory in a race at Delmar, California. Driving a P17 two-door sedan, Faulkner started on the outside of the sixth row in a twenty-three-car race. Faulkner was in second place by lap sixty and took the lead on lap ninety-eight when the leading Hudson ran out of gas. From 1949 through 1952, Plymouth was ranked number three in stock car wins across the country.

1950: More Of A Good Thing

At first glance it was easy to assume that Plymouth's 1950 offering was little more than a

The instrument panel was changed only slightly for 1950. Dark, rich, wood grain helped give the car an expensive look. *Ernest Fodor*

restyled 1949. Closer examination revealed that although the two cars were definitely siblings, a host of changes had taken place, so much so that only the doors were bolt-for-bolt interchanges between the two years. Basic contours remained the same, with relocated bolt holes and altered cut outs marking the differences between the two model years. As in 1949, Plymouth once again offered three distinct series on two different wheelbases. Model names remained the same, Deluxe and Special Deluxe, but engineering codes were changed to P19 for the short wheelbase Deluxe cars and P20 for the long wheelbase Deluxe and Special Deluxe. The switch from 1949 specifications was accomplished without any down time, the final 1949s rolling off the line November 25, 1949, followed by the first P20 Special Deluxes that same day. Switch over to the first

P19 Deluxe and P20 Deluxe took an additional ten days, the first of those coming off the line December 5.

The 111in wheelbase Deluxe line again included a fastback two-door sedan, a three-passenger business coupe, and the all-metal, two-door Suburban station wagon. The 118-1/2in wheelbase Deluxe line offered only a two-door club coupe and

The only true two-door sedan in Plymouth's 1950 line-up was this turtle back model, offered only on the 111in wheelbase P19 Deluxe chassis. The longer wheelbase car, though often referred to as a two door, was officially a "club coupe." Aftermarket sunvisor and fender skirts, along with later Plymouth wire wheels, dress up this example. Owner: Clyde McKinney.

four-door sedan, with the Special Deluxe offering those two body styles plus a convertible club coupe and four-door wood-bodied station wagon.

Distinguishing the 1950 cars from the 1949s were plain bumpers and a simplified stainless steel three-bar grille. The fluted, three-rib bumpers had been attractive but were expensive to manufacture and nearly impossible to straighten when dented. The new design, with a slight roll at the bottom edge of the face plate, helped the 1950 models appear more massive. The top bar of the grille curved to follow the grille cavity down to the front gravel shield. The center bar extended beyond the cavity to the outer edge of the fenders, as did the lower grille bar, both of which formed a boxed area for the now nearly square parking lamps. A single, center vertical bar served to accentuate the forward peak of the grille. The radiator badge was raised several inches from the leading edge of the hood line, with individual block letters spelling out "Plymouth" between the emblem and the edge of the hood. Viewed from the side, the cars looked nearly identical, though the rear bolt-on fenders were restyled and made slightly longer to give the car a more massive look on all models except the Suburban and woody wagon (which would retain the

1949-style fenders through the 1952 models). The rear fender stone shield was a bit larger, with less detail than before. Shortages of the fender shield found many cars built from August on shipped without them. Dealers were advised they would be shipped as soon as available and should be installed on cars already in the field, making it possible that some original cars were never fitted with them. The taillamps were in a horizontal format, moved down and wrapped around the fender rather than sitting on top of them as they had done in 1949. The separate trunk-mounted stop light used since 1941 was eliminated, both taillamps housing the brake and optional signal lamps under one lens.

The license plate light was placed above instead of below the license, and the old lever-style deck lid handle was now of the "T" variety. The rear nameplate was changed to a one-piece script and relocated above the license plate. There was little doubt that the car did look more massive, but the changes were so subtle it was hard to notice them. The rear window was 32 percent larger, curving around the edges further and set into its own self-locking rubber gasket. Early into production (P19 Deluxe 18061672, P20 Deluxe 15378781, and Special Deluxe 12446808), the cars were lowered 3/4in in

Convertibles continued to be among the lowest produced body styles. *Lee Dockery*

height by using different springs. This, combined with a wider tread stance, both front and rear, helped rid the car of its high and boxy look.

The front tread was increased from 55in to 55-7/16in by moving the center line of the wheel rim outward. The rear tread increase, from 56in to 58-7/16in, required a wider rear axle housing. The differential carrier and gearing remained the same as 1949, 3.73 for P19 models and 3.9 on all P20 models, with ratios of 3.9 and 4.1 optional, the 4.1 ratio standard on the wood body Special Deluxe station wagon. Despite the wider rear wheel tread, the box perimeter frame of the 1950 was the same as used under the 1949 models, with the exception of the Special Deluxe station wagon. P19 cars, with the exception of the Suburban, lacked a front sway bar, had only seven rear leaf springs, used a restriction thermostat, and did not come with an oil filter as standard equipment. Clutch plates in the P19 models were also 1/4in smaller (9-1/8in versus 9-1/4in) than those used in either the P20 Deluxe or Special Deluxe.

Interior choices were the same as in 1949, the only discernible change being new backgrounds of transparent gunmetal on spun aluminum for the gauges. The gunmetal finish was also used on the radio grille screen. The new rotary switches were retained, but larger control knobs helped make accessing them much easier. The beautiful wood-grain finish was retained on all models except the convertible, which continued to use a painted dashboard and garnish moldings as in years past. Business coupe buyers had a choice of vinyl resin or woven fiber fabric at no cost, with broadcloth optional. Deluxe two-door buyers had only a single choice of broadcloth with vinyl resin door trim. The P20 Deluxe club coupe and four-door sedan came in a single broadcloth choice, although buyers of the same body style in the P20 Special Deluxe version had a choice of blue or green broadcloth or blue or green pile fabric. Convertibles were finished in Bedford cord with vinyl resin trim at the top of the seats in either red, green, or blue, depending on the car's exterior color.

Sales of the all-metal Suburban station wagon continued to soar, despite grumbling from buyers that a more upscale model wasn't available. Realizing the potential for such a vehicle, a more upgraded version called the Special Suburban was added to the line. Identical in size to the standard Suburban, the Special Suburban had as standard equipment many items reserved for the P20 Special Deluxe cars, including armrests on both doors, assist straps and armrests in the rear compartment,

Leading sales once again was the Special Deluxe four-door sedan. Owner: Delane Patton.

glovebox lock, dual horns, horn ring, chrome radio grille, exterior belt line moldings, front bumper guards, chrome-plated tailgate hinges, and chrome rear window divider.

Special Suburban interiors were greatly upgraded, with rear sidewalls and wheel wells upholstered in pleated, brown, vinyl resin fabric. The headliner was done in brown checked woven fiber, with door panels in two tones of pleated brown vinyl and brown checked fabric. Like all P19 models, the Special Suburban rode on 6.40x15in tires. Unlike other P19s, the Suburbans were equipped with a front sway bar. Optional only on the Suburban were 6.00x18in wheels and tires. The Suburban wagons and Special Deluxe woody wagon shared a nine-leaf rear spring, compared to seven leaves on other P19 models and eight leaves on P20 Deluxe and Special Deluxe cars.

Outside of the increased rear axle width, mechanical changes were so few as to be almost nonexistent. An "improved" radiator core reduced coolant capacity from 15qt to 13-1/2qt. Cars built from August on were fitted with a narrower (3/8in versus 3/4in) fan belt and pulley. The electro-mechanical convertible power top motor, pump,

and reservoir were relocated (this change took place at the very end of 1949 production and can also be found on some P18 convertibles).

Motor Trend magazine road tested a Special Deluxe four door for its March issue and concluded it was "a car with riding comfort, handling ease and good visibility, although lacking in acceleration characteristics (0 to 60mph took 18.56sec to achieve). The reliability of any Chrysler product makes this car worthy of a prospective buyer's consideration." Model year production was up, but Plymouth's overall sales performance fell considerably, in what would be the best year the auto industry would see until 1955.

As a fuel economy champ, Plymouth was second only to the Ford six in the 1950 running of the Mobil Gas Economy Run. Plymouth recorded 21.25mpg against the winning Ford's 23.33mpg. In its traditional three-way race, Plymouth scored the lowest of either Ford or Chevrolet in the ton/miles per gallon category.

On the nation's race tracks, the pesky little Plymouths continued their winning ways. At the inaugural 500-mile race September 4 at Darlington, North Carolina, Johnny Mantz, driving a 1950 P19

Plymouth finally solved its spare tire problem with the 1949 models, mounting the tire in its own special alcove in the tailgate. The 1949 and 1950 wagons were also the first to have rear bumper overriders. The center section of the bumper had to be folded down before the tailgate could be opened. Owner: Ernest Fodor.

two-door sedan, outlasted the bigger, heavier cars to win the race at an average speed of 76.26mph. The Mantz car, which was later wrecked, has been replicated and is on display at the Speedway to this day Museum. Walt Faulkner campaigned his 1950 Plymouth to a second-place finish in the 250-lap Oakland (California) Speedway race, one of nine cars out of twenty still running at the race's end. Fourth place went to another Plymouth. At the Carrell (California) Speedway, George Seeger placed third driving a 1949 in that 250-lap race. At the Oakland Classic on October 1, Plymouths placed fourth, fifth and sixth in a 300-lap contest. Wilkesboro, North Carolina's, 100-Mile Grand National Race on September 24 saw Plymouths come in first, second, fourth, fifth, sixth, and seventh—the winning driver, Leon Sales of Winston-Salem, driving the same car Mantz drove to victory at Darlington. In Hillsboro, North Carolina, October 29, Lee Petty, who had started it all, was declared the winner (at 175 miles) of the 200-mile NASCAR race on the Occoneechee track. Averaging 92.7mph in his 1950 Plymouth business coupe, the race had to be called because of darkness!

Plymouth's last wood-body station wagon was built in 1950. U.S. Body & Forging, known now as Ushco Manufacturing, had been Plymouth's sole station wagon body supplier since the first "official" station wagon back in 1934. Sales of wood-body wagons had continued to dwindle, down to just 2,057 units for 1950. The woody wagon not only cost more to buy, it was an expensive body to maintain. Plymouth recommended the wood work be revarnished every six to eight months when exposed to excessive sunlight or salty air conditions. The trouble-free all-metal Suburban, despite having only two doors and a limited carrying capacity, had easily spelled the woody wagon's doom. The all-metal wagons lacked only one ingredient—they never had the class associated with the wooden-bodied cars. What they lacked in class they more than made up for in sales, accounting for 5.6 percent of sales in 1950, compared to the wood wagons' 0.34 percent. Plymouth dealers were advised in September that any further orders for wood body parts would no longer be sent to Ushco, but would be supplied directly through the regular Chrysler parts outlets, a complete change in procedure from years past. The list sent to dealers included parts for only the P15, P18 and P20 woody wagons. The end of an era had come to the station wagon business.

As Plymouth steamed head-on into its best sales year since 1937, the U.S. found itself embroiled in another overseas conflict following Communist North Korea's invasion of South Korea. There were justifiable concerns Korea would drag the country back into another world war. As had been the case during World War II, the government began placing restrictions on the automobile indus-

IMPORTANT NOTICE ON THE CARE OF CHROMIUM PLATING

In the interest of the National Defense Program, industry-wide restrictions on the use of nickel have made necessary a change in the chromium plating of the various interior and exterior trim parts of your beautiful new Chrysler.

As we know it is your desire to maintain the original beautiful appearance of this new chromium finish, simple instructions for its care are outlined in your Owner Manual under "Retaining That Original Showroom Look."

Your Chrysler dealer will be only too glad to advise you fully on the care required for this finish or will provide this care, if you so desire.

CHRYSLER SALES DIVISION

As the Korean Conflict placed more and more restrictions on strategic materials, chrome plating became ever thinner. Owners found this flyer in the glovebox along with the owners manual.

Plymouth in Canada
by Lanny Knutson
Very Similar Yet Subtly Different

The same phrase that aptly compares the neighboring populations of the United States and Canada, can also apply to the Plymouth automobiles each country produced. At first blush they seem identical, but the more one checks under the surface, the more differences one finds.

Plymouth came to Canada in the same manner it arrived on the American scene. When Walter P. Chrysler took over the troubled Maxwell-Chalmers company, its Canadian subsidiary came along with the deal, including a Windsor, Ontario, factory Maxwell Motor Company of Canada had built in 1918.

First organized as the Maxwell-Chrysler Co. of Canada, the new company was reorganized on June 17, 1925, and named the Chrysler Corporation of Canada Ltd (a name that remained in use until 1963 when it was shortened to Chrysler Canada Ltd).

The old Windsor Maxwell factory, although it remained in use into the 1980s, never housed its progeny's assembly line. The first Plymouths were produced in a new factory built on farmland in nearby Walkerville. That area is now incorporated into the city of Windsor and the plant remains as the nucleus of Chrysler Canada's Windsor Assembly Plant.

The Postwar Years

The Chrysler Corporation of Canada wasted little time getting into automotive production once WWII hostilities ceased in 1945. By that year's end a dozen Plymouths had already been produced.

As in the U.S. the new 1946 Plymouths were basically warmed-over 1942s with minor changes and some Canadian differences. One difference was in model selection. While the U.S. Deluxe and Special Deluxe series both offered a full and nearly identical compliment of body styles (except for the convertible and the wood station wagon which were available in Special Deluxe form only), each Canadian Plymouth series had its own unique body style. Beginning in 1942 and continuing through 1948 the Deluxe series was only available as a business coupe or two-door sedan while the Special Deluxe series exclusively marketed a club coupe and four-door sedan. Only four body styles were offered; two in each series.

The 1949 model year brought the first true postwar Plymouth to Canada as it did to the United States. Beginning with this year, Canada offered all Plymouth models and body styles with the exception of the convertible and the wood station wagon. The new, all-steel, 111in wheelbase P17 wagon was available in any Canadian Plymouth color, while in the U.S. it initially could be had in any color the customer wanted as long as it was brown.

As in the past, luxury models such as the convertible and station wagon could be purchased in Canada but they had to be imported, often with a sizeable surcharge that only wealthier customers could afford.

In 1953, the U.S. Plymouth's horsepower increased to 100 while the Canadian's stayed at 97hp. In 1954, both Plymouths took their respective corporations' Dodge motors (230.2ci for the United States, 228.1ci for Canada).

The short, side window club coupe was the only pillared two-door available in the Canadian Plymouth line for 1953–54. The two-door sedan with the longer roof was not offered (although erroneously illustrated in the Canadian catalog).

As the 1953 model year began, the Belvedere became Canada's first Plymouth hardtop. By midyear it was joined by a Belvedere four-door sedan. Interestingly, Canada's top sedan was offered at a higher trim level than any available in the U.S. In addition to the hard-top's nameplates and C-pillar trim being applied to the sedan, a chrome spear, tapered at both ends, was added to the front doors. Although it looked rather like the add-on it was, the spear was a low-cost imitation of the hardtop's full-length molding. The Belvedere sedan's interior also came standard with full carpeting, special upholstery patterns and a two-tone dash treatment. On the exterior, backup lights were incorporated into shortened taillight lenses. This Canadian Belvedere sedan was a forerunner to the full Belvedere line that would appear in 1954 on both sides of the border.

Canada's 1954 Belvedere catalog also included a domestically offered convertible for the first time. Although still imported, a convertible was at least easier to get.

The deluxe Suburban was a Savoy (rather than a Belvedere) model in Canada. Otherwise, with the exclusion of the two-door sedan, the model/body lineups were the same on both sides of the border.

The all-new 1955 Plymouths offered V-8 power for the first time to both Canadian and American buyers. However, it was available only in the Canadian Belvedere line, and, consequently, the six still outsold the new V-8. For Powerflite-equipped Canadian Plymouths, the former Chrysler Spitfire 251ci engine was employed. Surprisingly this six was 10ci larger than the new 241ci V-8, although at 125 bhp, it produced less horsepower than the V-8. The 260ci American Plymouth V-8 was unavailable in Canada.

The first Canadian-produced convertible was offered by Plymouth in 1955. No three-passenger business coupe was marketed in Canada. The Plaza wagon came only as a two-door, but the Savoy line offered both a four-door Suburban and a two-door hardtop. The latter could be mistaken for a Belvedere because it (and the Savoy sedans) could be had with the top line's Sportone treatment. Offering a higher trim level in a lower priced car it was another Canadian variation.

In 1956, the Belvedere was a V-8 line only, coming standard with the new-to-Canada 270ci motor. The 251ci six was standard in manual transmission as well as Powerflite-equipped Plazas and Savoys.

A four-door hardtop joined the Belvedere line, and a Plaza (business coupe) was offered this one year only, although it would be offered in the U.S. through 1959.

The new Fury was not available in Canada even though its 303 engine (a hopped-up version of Canada's "big" Dodge Coronet V-8) was produced in the Canadian factory.

The 303 engine became the standard Plymouth V-8 in 1957 but in its mild, original Canadian form. It was larger, however, than the standard American Plymouth V-8 engine. The big 251 six continued, this time pushing out 132hp.

Canada's version of the sensational Flight-Sweep-styled 1957 Plymouth came in most of the variations offered in the U.S. Missing were the Plaza business coupe, the Savoy four-door hardtop, and the Fury.

The Savoy hardtop sedan joined Canada's 1958 Plymouth lineup and some reports claim that the Fury did too, available only with the new 350ci B-block rather than the "standard" high-performance 318 of the American version.

The 318, so familiar stateside, would not be offered in Canada until 1965. In its place was an identical-appearing 313ci engine created by boring the 303. It produced five fewer horsepower than the American 318.

Fury definitely came to the Canadian Plymouth line in 1959, but, as in the U.S., it was the downgraded Fury offered in both four and two doors. The Sport Fury was not built in Canada but could be imported.

The flathead six, in its final automotive season, remained at 251ci but its horsepower was increased to 135bhp. Two V-8s were offered, both 313s. The standard version came with a two-barrel carb; optional was a four-barrel, dual exhaust, Power-Pak version. No B-block V-8 was available.

Nineteen fifty-nine marked the end of three Plymouth traditions, two shared with its American counterpart: the flathead six, separate body-frame construction, and bodies supplied to Dodge. Future Canadian differences would be even more subtle, but they'd still be there!

This convertible has accessory guards around the door handles. These were a late addition to the option list and could be fitted to cars as far back as the 1949 models. The wire wheels on this car are incorrect, as they weren't offered until 1953. Owner: Philip Johnson.

try. By October steel was in short supply, as were other critical materials such as chromium and copper. For a time it appeared the government might have to once again curtail automobile production. For Plymouth in general and Chrysler Corporation as a whole, these events would end up turning against the company. Ford Motor Company was under new management and breathing hard down Chrysler's neck to regain its number-two position in the automobile industry. More worrisome was Buick, which was openly aiming to wrestle third place away from Plymouth. Despite a reduction in market share, sales of over 600,000 cars set an all-time record for Plymouth, which would remain the number-three selling automobile for 1950. But the market was changing– would Plymouth change to keep up? Unfortunately its continued sales successes may have lulled corporate thinking into a false sense of security.

1951: The Year That Almost Wasn't

For Plymouth, 1951 could have been the year that almost didn't happen. Korea may have been termed just a "police action," but its effect on the automobile industry nearly rivaled that of World War II. What had started as a record-breaking production pace led to fears fueled by National Production Authority warnings (which never materialized) that by mid-year a 50 percent production cutback–or even total shut down–might occur. All manufacturers were affected by restrictions on steel, aluminum, copper, nickel, zinc, cobalt, and cadmium. Strikes–both real and threatened–along with unclear governmental policies helped keep the industry in turmoil throughout the year. As one of the nation's prime government contractors, Chrysler Corporation was committed to providing technical personnel and production facilities for military purposes at the expense of domestic automobile production.

Despite these obstacles, Plymouth entered the 1951 market with, if not three completely new models, at least three new model names. Abandoning the term "Deluxe" (which had been used since 1933) and "Special Deluxe" (used since 1941), the new models were called Concord, Cambridge, and Cranbrook. Engineering codes continued to add confusion to the line-up–the Concord, which replaced the 111in wheelbase Deluxe cars, was known as the Model P22. Why the numbers didn't

Marketplace(Calendar Year 1951)
Chevrolet–21.1 percent
Ford–16.9 percent
Plymouth–11.4 percent

Club coupe sales helped to make them the second most popular after the four-door sedan. This is the P20 Deluxe version. Owner: Charles Geissler.

increment in numerical order (using P21) has never been explained. The Cambridge, engineering code P23S, replaced the 118-1/2in wheelbase Deluxe line, with the Cranbrook, model P23C, replacing the Special Deluxe. The first Cranbrooks rolled off the line December 11, only nine days after the last P20 Special Deluxe. The first Cambridge followed the next day, with Concord production starting a day later. Before the end of the model year, Plymouth would celebrate building its 7 millionth automobile.

The names may have been new, but body styles were unchanged. Concord buyers had a choice of a three-passenger business coupe, a fastback two-door sedan, or an all-metal two-door Suburban station wagon (the upscale version was called Savoy).

The Cambridge offered only a club coupe and four-door sedan. The Cranbrook was offered in club coupe; four-door sedan; convertible club coupe; and, new for the year, Cranbrook Belvedere "hardtop convertible" body styles. Unlike the real convertible with folding top, the "hardtop" convertible had a fixed roof with pillarless side windows like those used on the convertible.

The Cranbrook Belvedere was Plymouth's answer to Chevrolet's highly successful Bel Air hardtop introduced the year before. Chrysler Corporation had originated the first two-door hardtop bodies back in 1946, building a handful of Town & Country hardtops. For whatever reason, the body style was shelved, only to be resurrected in 1949 by both Buick and Cadillac. Chevrolet's version, the Bel Air, forced both Plymouth and Ford (with the Victoria) to enter the market with similar body styles for the 1951 season.

Distinguishing the 1951 Plymouth from its predecessors was a new front end ensemble, marked by a sloping hood and new grille. The grille was lower and wider, with the upper bar sloping out further under the headlights before turning down to meet the smaller parking lamps that were now mounted on the bar, rather than being surrounded by it. A heavy center bar floated across the middle of the grille cavity and carried three massive vertical teeth, the two outer teeth riding behind similarly shaped bumper overriders. The lip that had previously run along the bottom of the bumper face plate was eliminated. The hood front sloped back sharply, in contrast to the vertical hood fronts of 1949–50. The familiar Mayflower sailing ship sat further back on the hood, "speed waves" flowing outward from the ship's base. The shield-shaped medallion was restyled and located above the lower hood plate, which now contained the word "Plymouth" in red on a chrome lip. Wheel opening cutouts were squared off, accentuated by a spear of stainless trim running from the headlamp back to the front door. A similar stainless spear and "gracefully simple" stone shields adorned the rear fenders. Front fender ornamentation included name badges signifying the model series. As restrictions on chrome became more stringent, many normally chrome-plated trim pieces such as parking and taillight bezels, headlamp rims, name plates, and license plate housings were all coated with a colorless enamel.

The deck lid was revised only slightly, with the ornamentation rearranged to distinguish the 1951 from earlier cars (the deck lid itself interchanged with 1949–50 cars). The windshield size was increased by narrowing the front "A" pillars—windshields were still two pieces of flat glass, a much ballyhooed economy measure in Plymouth advertising, as were the bolt-on rear fenders that had long since been abandoned by the competition.

The most dramatic changes were made to the instrument panel. The modernized panel located all the gauges directly in front of the driver in one grouping, the dark horizontal wood grain replaced by a lighter, vertically-grained finish that did little to accentuate the car's interior. The radio nestled at the top center of the dash, with the speaker grille following the downward slope of the panel and stopping just short of the heater control panel. A removable medallion to the right of the radio allowed for installation of a clock, with a sliding-drawer ash tray located directly beneath. Other changes included a larger steering wheel hub to house "built-in" turn signals, moving the combination ignition-starter switch to the right of the steering column, and changing the emergency brake handle from a pistol grip to a "T" handle. Plymouth buyers finally got electric windshield wipers as standard equipment, something the other Chrysler lines had for many years.

Upholstery patterns were new, with broadcloth standard on the Concord business coupe as well as the two-door sedan. Regular Suburbans continued to use vinyl, although the Savoy came in Bedford cord with vinyl trim like the convertible. Cambridges were upholstered in broadcloth with Cranbrooks offered in either broadcloth or Herringbone Weave to harmonize with the body color.

Suburban sales continued to soar, despite the lack of a four-door station wagon, but the big news for the year was the addition of the Cranbrook Belvedere hardtop convertible. The Belvedere buyer had his choice of blue or green striped broadcloth or striped Herringbone weave with vinyl resin trim to harmonize with the exterior body colors. The Belvedere could be had in any of eight solid colors, and for the first time since 1941, four two-tone combinations (Cranbrook club coupe and four-door sedans built after June could also be two-toned.) Like other hardtops of the period, the body structure of the Belvedere was pure convertible, sharing the same doors, deck lid, and trim items—only the fixed roof and three-piece rear window were different.

Under the sheet metal the 1951 Plymouths were boringly the same—the engine was still a 217ci six rated at 97hp. In mid-April steel asbestos cylinder head gaskets replaced copper gaskets, and engines that had traditionally been painted aluminum were painted gray due to a scarcity of aluminum paint. The only transmission was a three-speed manual, running through a single-plate clutch to a Hotchkiss rear end. Centrifuse brake drums, Oilite fuel tank filter, automatic electric choke, boxed perimeter frame, tapered rear leaf springs, and other mechanicals were carryovers, with the exception of pressurized radiator caps and "Safety Flow

Ride" Oriflow shock absorbers. Oriflow shocks were designed to vary their resistance, by hydraulic flow control, in proportion to the severity of the impulses to the suspension. Off the car, if the rod was pulled slowly the shock would extend quite easily–try to do it fast and it became an impossible task. Motorists not familiar with how Oriflow shocks worked were suckered into purchasing new shocks by unscrupulous service station owners who would slowly and easily push the bumper of the car in the "standard" shock absorber test–the Oriflow shock would allow the car to bounce up and down–just as a normal worn out shock would do.

Plymouth continued to be a major supplier to taxi cab fleets, offering a package that included a 10in clutch, commercial duty chassis springs, firm ride shock absorbers, heavier gauge springs in seats and seatbacks, battery heat shield, and heavy-duty 100amp-hour battery. The taxi package was also recommended for Suburban models if they would be expected to carry heavy loads like power tools or be used as delivery vehicles. Standard tires on the Suburbans (and other Concord models) were 6.40x15in Goodyears. For the first time, 6.70x15in Super Cushion tires were offered as options on Suburbans and were recommended when carrying heavier loads. When fitted with the 6.70 tire, the normal axle ratio of 3.73 was replaced by 3.9 gearing. High-clearance 18in wheels remained an exclusive Suburban option.

Plymouth's 97hp "weaklings" continued to be the scourge of the NASCAR tracks, muscling their way in among the more high-powered V-8 Oldsmobiles and "Twin H Power" Hudson Hornets. Fifty-two Plymouth race cars were registered with NASCAR (second in number only to Ford); in year end standings, Plymouth came in second behind leading Oldsmobile (which had thirty-seven cars

The grille featured three vertical bars, but the outer two were hidden by the bumper overriders. The Plymouth shield rode below the Mayflower ship. Owner: Anton Skadberg.

The dashboard was grained in a lighter, vertical pattern; 1951 would be the last year for wood-grained dashboards. *Jim Benjaminson*

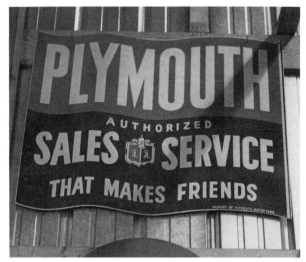

A Plymouth sign from the early 1950s. *Jim Benjaminson*

1951 Concord managed only 24.145mpg—the lowest actual mileage recorded by any of the four cars in the class—but was declared second-place winner for its ton/mpg rating of 48.954. The winning car, a Nash Rambler, scored 31.05mpg and 53.489 ton-miles.

As the war in Korea continued to divert needed materials from the industry, the car's quality began to suffer. Chrome plating took on a dingy look, as first copper and then nickel were eliminated from the plating process by government regulation (quality chrome plating consists of three layers, first copper, then nickel, and finally chromium). Copper shortages also affected the availability of radios and heaters. Interestingly, all cars were still being shipped with five tires, though whitewalls were not available. Steel production in the second quarter was 20 percent below that of the first half of 1950, forcing most manufacturers to cancel or delay introductions of their 1952 car lines. Those who had planned new models, like Plymouth, were forced to make due with what they had for one more year. For a time it appeared that rationing of new automobiles or curtailment of production altogether was possible if the industry was called back into service.

As fears of all out war spread, the automobile industry looked to the federal government for advice. Washington politicians felt Detroit's giant

registered) with two first-, nine second-, twelve third-, ten fourth- and eleven fifth-place finishes.

Plymouth didn't fare nearly as well in the 1951 running of the Mobil Gas Economy Run, a Cranbrook placing fourth (of five entries) in Class A, scoring 22.99mpg. Class champion was a Ford V-8, followed by a Studebaker Champion and a Ford six. In the "Special Lightweight 6-cylinder Class" a

This double-ended 1951 Plymouth was displayed for many years at the Horseless Carriage Museum in Rapid City, South Dakota. The car can now be seen at the Pioneer Auto Museum at Murdo, South Dakota. *Brian Crane*

manufacturing plants should be dispersed around the country, fearing that an atomic bomb strike would cripple U.S. war efforts. Steel shortages forced all manufacturers to cut back, yet the government refused to release orders for military production. Only Chrysler's Newark, Delaware, plant was committed to military production, building tanks.

A fourteen-week strike early in the 1951 model year added further to the industry's misery, and it wasn't until a threatened national railroad strike in May that the government stepped in to intervene. Chrysler Corporation testified before the U.S. Senate in September that if it didn't get more steel, there was a distinct possibility it would have to shut down entirely. Fears of massive unemployment due to industry layoffs went unheeded as the government refused to provide the industry with guidelines. For a time it appeared 1952 models would be canceled entirely. It was January 1952 before they did make their appearance; V-8 engines for both

Dodge and DeSoto were early casualties of production cutbacks.

The National Production Authority was charged with allocating how many cars each manufacturer would be allowed to build during this period. Chrysler Corporation's allocation of 1,242,256 vehicles was well above that of Ford (1,115,440) but far below GM's allocation of 2,121,980 cars for 1951. At year's end Chrysler had built 1,227,475 vehicles, while Ford and GM exceeded their allocations by 50,700 and 145,000 vehicles respectively.

The industry was further rocked by Federal Regulation W, which required new and used car buyers to put down one-third cash and pay off the remaining balance on automobile loans within 15 months. Regulation W requirements meant monthly payments averaging $80 to $110, far beyond the reach of most potential customers. Production, which had been running at near record levels until W took effect, took a nose dive. During the first seven days of its implementation, sales of new cars

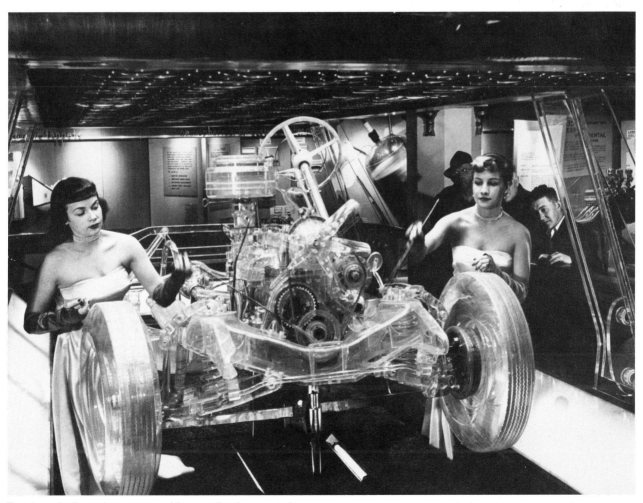

The clear plastic engine was operable, revealing how an automobile engine works. Some internal engine parts were painted in fluorescent colors. *Chrysler Historical Foundation*

fell more than 50 percent in the Detroit area alone. Used car sales fared even worse, with a 60 percent drop. During the first month of Regulation W, orders for 2,375 new cars and 865 used cars were canceled just in the city of Chicago. Hardest hit by Regulation W were medium- and high-price car manufacturers, such as Kaiser-Frazer, who were forced to completely revamp production schedules to build more inexpensive (and less profitable) models—exactly opposite of what Kaiser needed to do if it was to remain a viable competitor.

Despite war jitters and Regulation W, Chrysler, Ford, and General Motors all marched ahead with plans to expand. Ford's plant construction would increase its capacity by 50 percent, a move that would prove disastrous to Plymouth as Ford and Chevrolet engaged in an all-out sales war during 1953 to 1954. Buick reached an all-time high of more than 500,000 cars and had tooling in place to better that figure—openly announcing its goal "to supplant Plymouth as the third largest producer."

Chrysler purchased 3,800 acres of land fifty miles west of Detroit, near Chelsea, Michigan, where it began building, under the direction of A.B. "Tobe" Couture, its own proving ground. Ground was also broken for a 650,000sq-ft factory in Indiana where it was correctly rumored that Chrysler would begin building automatic transmissions for Plymouth. More than half the new cars sold in 1951 were equipped with automatics, a fact not lost

Plymouth spent eighteen months building this clear plastic car for the show circuit. *Chrysler Historical Foundation*

on Plymouth marketing (Chevrolet and Ford offered an automatic). Rumors throughout the industry saw Chevrolet and Plymouth bringing out V-8 engines as soon as possible–the unavailability of machine tools prevented either from achieving this goal for at least three years–nonetheless Chrysler began construction of a new engine plant twenty-five miles east of Detroit.

In the Chrysler board room, K.T. Keller resigned as president to move up to the board of directors and chairmanship of Chrysler's guided missile program for the Armed Forces. Keller–and Chrysler–had been deeply involved in the Manhattan Project during WWII, which resulted in development of the atomic bomb (how involved the corporation had been has never been completely revealed). Replacing Keller at the helm of Chrysler was L.L. Colbert, a long-time corporate executive. J.P. Mansfield, who would later head the Plymouth Division, was elected a vice-president of the corporation and director of Plymouth. (Death claimed two Chrysler Corporation pioneers during the year–Fred Zeder passing away in February and Joseph Fields in March.)

K.T. Keller had been many things to Chrysler, and a man on whom much blame has been laid over the years for the solid, but rather stodgy, products turned out by the corporation in the early 1950s. Keller has been sorely overlooked as the man who hired a young Studebaker stylist named Virgil Exner to turn the corporation's styling fortunes around. Plymouth–and Chrysler–would face some rocky times in the near future, but a new era was dawning for the nation's number-three automobile.

1952: Subtle Changes

Despite continued shortages and threats of a nationwide steel strike (averted by President Truman's seizure of the steel industry April 8, 1952), cars built to 1952 specifications began rolling off the lines in November 1951 though the official announcement date wouldn't come until January. The 1952 Plymouth boasted "forty-six advances" though few were readily apparent. To the casual observer, the 1952 Plymouth looked identical to the 1951 models. Unlike the 1946–1949 P15 Plymouth, which had been virtually unchanged for three years, there were external trim changes to differentiate the 1952s from the 1951s.

From the front, the hood medallion was the most obvious change, now round instead of shield

While it took a good eye to distinguish a 1952 from a 1951, the Cranbrook Belvedere hardtop convertible was easily identified by the extended two-tone paint which dropped from the roof over the rear quarters and deck lid. Owner: Dale Reinke.

shaped. The Mayflower ship hood ornament sat lower and looked more like a ship than a plane, the "bow waves" from 1951 having been eliminated. The grille, headlamps, parking lamps, bumpers, and overriders were identical to previous models. The front fender name plates were in script, rather than block lettering, providing the only clues as to the model year when the car was viewed in profile. Around back, the Plymouth nameplate was moved down with the letters becoming part of the license plate light ornament. Taillights, rear bumper, and overriders were carried over from 1951.

These changes were considered so minimal that Plymouth chose to carry over the same engineering codes and model names. Serial number sequences were not consecutive as was done with the P15s, although the numbers were bumped only slightly to provide positive identification between the 1951 P22/P23 cars and the 1952 versions. Ten body styles were again offered–the 111in wheelbase Concord available in three-passenger business coupe, two-door fastback sedan, or all-metal Suburban station wagon. The Savoy continued as the upscale version of the wagon. Cambridge buyers were offered the club coupe and four-door sedan on the

118-1/2in chassis, with Cranbrook buyers opting for a club coupe, four-door, convertible club coupe, or the Cranbrook Belvedere convertible hardtop.

The Cranbrook Belvedere, although basically the same car as before, was the only body style different enough to recognize at a distance by virtue of its new roof and paint treatment. The side window drip molding, rather than stopping at the belt line molding, swept down behind the quarter window, crossed over the belt line, then flowed down the fender-body seam (rear fenders were still detachable) to the rear bumper. When two toned, the color of the top cascaded across the deck lid as well, the moldings serving as the dividing line between the two colors. A "Belvedere" script was placed between the molding and belt line. The Cranbrook Belvedere was painted in one standard color, a metallic "Belmont Blue." Two-tone combinations, of which there were three, were optional. Cranbrook Belvedere upholstery combinations included blue, black-gray, or beige textured weave fabric with gray, green, or tan vinyl trim.

Two-tone paints were still available by special order on Cranbrook club coupe and four-door sedans, although few cars seem to have been sold with the option. Only one color–Dawn Gray–was used on the upper body, with choices of Belmont Blue, Wedgewood, or Lido Green on the lower body.

Interior changes for 1952 were limited to new upholstery materials in closed cars, the instrument panel now finished in a solid "Lustre Tone" (Alaska Gray Metallic) finish instead of woodgraining. The speedometer face was slightly different, the gauges using a black on white versus white on black background. A larger speedometer needle drew com-

The most popular 1952 model was the Cranbrook four-door sedan. Nineteen fifty-two models were late in getting into dealer showrooms, as fears of escalated fighting in Korea nearly kept them from being built. Owner: Tom Erovick. *Jim Benjaminson*

Chrome-plated tailgate hinges added some sparkle to the rear of the 1951–52 Savoy Suburban. Owner: Fred Long.

plaints from various road test personnel when it was found the needle obscured several numerals at one time, making it hard to distinguish the exact speed at which the car was traveling. Marking one more difference was the steering wheel ship ornament, which was set against a black background instead of red. Signal lights were optional, and on cars so equipped a single green indicator did not distinguish between right or left.

Cambridge and Concord cars were upholstered in a neutral textured fabric weave, while Cranbrook closed cars had blue or green textured weave, depending on the outer body color. Suburban wagons continued to use vinyl except in the upscale Savoy wagon, which had blue or red striped Bedford Cord with matching vinyl trim in a style similar to the convertible club coupe. It offered Bedford Cord with blue or black vinyl trim or maroon Bedford with maroon vinyl bolsters.

Radio grilles were installed in all Cranbrook body styles and the Savoy from January 1952 on, with the grille painted in Alaska Gray Metallic to match the instrument panel. Radio installations in the Cambridge, Concord, or Suburban required that a speaker grille package be installed in addition to the radio. Although the speaker grilles were

the same for both years, the 1951 grille was wood grained and had to be painted before being installed in 1952 cars. An unseen but appreciated change was higher-speed electric windshield wipers; owners had complained that the slow sweep of the earlier wipers was hypnotic.

A new cylinder head provided a change in combustion chamber design, resulting in improved performance, though the 97hp rating remained the same as the 1949–51 cars. This head (with part number 1405849 embossed on it) could be retrofitted back through the P15 models. Motor Vehicle Research drivers, testing a Cranbrook four door in the June 1952 issue of *Science and Mechanics*, reported they had tried in vain to make the engine ping, starting up a hill in low gear, then quickly dropping the car into high and loading it.

Motor Vehicle Research wanted to find out why "cost-conscious cab fleet owners favor a car whose initial cost is not the lowest in its class" (according to a survey, 57 percent of all standard taxi cabs registered were Plymouths). Conducting their tests in 40deg January weather they recorded gas mileage figures of 21–22mpg in the 20–30mph range, dropping to 19–21mpg at 30–40mph. At 70mph, mileage dropped to a dismal 12.75mpg.

The Concord business coupe proved to be popular with salesmen. Owner: Phil Lee.

The Mayflower still looked like a ship. *Jim Benjaminson*

Among the few changes for 1952 was the circular radiator medallion containing the Mayflower. Owner: Alf Jacob Munthe.

Other tests recorded attainable top speed as 92 "uncorrected" mph, with 0–60mph "through the gears" in slightly better than 21sec.

Plymouth hydraulic brakes were a shining spot of the test, achieving 96 percent efficiency at 40mph, 80 percent at 50mph, and 67 percent at 60mph–all panic stops. One of Plymouth's unseen changes for 1952 was Cyclebond brake shoes, which eliminated the use of rivets in securing the linings to the shoes.

Motor Vehicle Research testers concluded that Plymouth offered rugged (rather than rapid) performance, ease of serviceability, comfortable seats, and excellent vision in all directions. April 1952's *Motor Trend* called it "a remarkably honest piece of merchandise, but high-priced for what it has to offer the buyer."Best ride of the economy cars, fine brakes, plus top economy were among the finest traits noted by *Motor Trend. Motor Trend*'s test car hit a high speed of 88mph with fuel consumption figures of 23.2mpg at a steady 30mph, 20.9mpg at 45mph, and 17.3mpg at 60mph. *Motor Trend* drivers ran the 0–60mph test in 22.54sec, considerably slower than the 18.56sec recorded for the 1950 Plymouth they had tested .

Drivers Eddie Bishop and Bill Cameron piloted a Cranbrook and Concord in the 1952 Mobil Gas Economy Run, with Cameron's Cranbrook edging out the Concord by nearly a 1/2mpg–23.522mpg vs. 23.079. Neither mark was good enough for top honors–the two Plymouths placing ninth and tenth behind two Studebaker V-8s, a Ford Mainline six, a Mercury Monterey (declared the overall winner by virtue of its 59.71ton/mpg rating), a Kaiser, and a pair of Henry J Corsairs, one a six and the other a four (and overall gas mileage champ at 30.855mpg).

In the ton-mile rating the Concord placed fifteenth to the Cranbrook's nineteenth place finish.

Motor Vehicle Research drivers found the 1952 Cranbrook to be tight and quiet while *Motor Trend* complained of excessive wind noises that had to be repaired by the dealer. *Motor Trend* also complained of quality control, citing items as the steering wheel spokes not sitting "square" when the car was driven in a straight line. Quality control complaints were not common with these cars–one explanation may be the *Motor Trend* car could have been built in one of the two California assembly plants, Los Angeles or San Leandro, while the Motor Vehicle Research car (whose tests were conducted in New Hampshire) was probably built in Detroit.

Of the three low-priced cars, Plymouth was the only one to offer the ubiquitous three-speed manual as the only choice of transmission. Chevrolet had a choice of manual or (since 1950) Power Glide automatic while Ford offered manual, manual with overdrive, and (since 1951) Ford-o-matic automatic transmissions. Chrysler Corporation engineers, working with Borg-Warner, developed an overdrive transmission in 1934, installing it in Chrysler and DeSoto Airflows. Having pioneered the use of overdrive, Chrysler made little use of it–Chrysler and DeSoto offered it through 1940 on 6-cylinder cars and in 1941 straight-8s. Between 1935 and 1942 eight other automakers jumped on the overdrive bandwagon using the same Borg-Warner unit, but it wasn't until mid-1952 that Chrysler saw fit to make it available on Plymouth and Dodge, and reintroduce it on the DeSoto. Dodge and DeSoto would offer overdrive through 1956, while Plymouth would retain it through 1959. In contrast, Ford and Mercury offered overdrive from 1949 through 1963 and Chevrolet (the only GM user) from 1955 to 1963.

The overdrive unit was essentially a small case bolted behind the standard three-speed transmission, having a planetary gearset that, when engaged, reduced engine revs by 30 percent. Fully automatic, electrically operated overdrives were first introduced in 1939 and appeared in their final, simplified, and less bulky form in 1946. The Plymouth overdrive provided "fourth gear" performance at speeds above 25mph. The overdrive unit drove the propeller shaft ten revolutions for every seven revolutions of the engine. (Plymouth cars shipped to overseas markets had been fitted–from Detroit–with overdrive transmissions as far back as 1936.)

Operation of the overdrive was simple, being controlled by the accelerator pedal. To achieve "kick down" to obtain added acceleration the driver depressed the accelerator pedal to the wide open position. This de-energized the electric solenoid, releasing engine torque brought about by a temporary interruption of ignition allowing the control pawl in the overdrive to release, placing the unit in direct drive. Engagement could be done at any time by lifting the foot from the accelerator pedal. The overdrive unit could be disengaged permanently by following the same procedure and pulling out the control handle located on the dash. Under 20mph lock out could be accomplished simply by pulling the handle out without having to lift off the accelerator. Despite being made available midway into the model year, overdrive found its way into only 17 percent of Plymouth's production.

Overdrive proved popular enough that Plymouth offered it as a complete service package to be installed in the field on P22 and P23 series cars. Net dealer price, which included the overdrive and mainshaft assembly, clutch disc, hand brake drum, wiring harness, and necessary controls was $142.25. First shipments of the kit were not scheduled until mid-May 1952. For owners of earlier Plymouths, the unit was virtually a bolt-in swap for cars dating back to 1940. As early as 1940, Plymouth had used a long tailshaft assembly on their transmissions. Removing this tailshaft allowed the overdrive unit to slip into its place, allowing the original drive shaft to be used.

Standard tire size on the Suburban and Savoy station wagons was changed to 6.70x15in and the rear axle ratio to 3.9 like the full-size Cambridge and Cranbrook models. The Concord continued to use 6.40x15in tires and a 3.73 axle ratio. When equipped with overdrive, rear-end ratios were changed on all models: to 4.1 on the Concord

Plymouth lumped 1951 and 1952 production figures together making it impossible to tell how many convertibles were built each year—this 1952 had different deck lid trim to differentiate it from the 1951. Owner: Tom Mansfield.

coupe and two door, and 4.3 on all Cambridge, Cranbrook, Suburbans, and Savoys. The Suburbans, when equipped with the 18in high clearance wheels, received a 4.78 ratio.

Korean War restrictions continued to plague the production lines–copper head gaskets continued to be replaced by steel and "steelbestos" gaskets. Fuel pump heat shields were eliminated after the fuel pump was redesigned. Surprisingly, despite these material restrictions, whitewall tires became available in May. Government restrictions controlling the amount of nickel used in chrome-plating were still in effect and owners found a one-page leaflet in the glove compartment advising them to

The Cranbrook convertible is a rare car today. Owner: Gloria Svenson.

read the owners manual for instructions on how to protect the colorless, baked-on enamel protective coating on these pieces. Even paint colors continued to be affected–Sable Bronze (used in Belvedere two-tone combinations) was lightened, just as Empire Maroon had replaced the slightly darker Mecca Maroon in July 1951. Nineteen-fifty-one also saw two shades of Niles Green, one metallic, the other non-metallic.

New to the accessory list was tinted "Solex" glass. One of Plymouth's more popular accessories did not debut until spring 1952, when MoPar door handle guards came on the market. Made of polished stainless steel, the guards fit under the door handles (they had to be removed to install them) and protected the paint against ring and key scratches. These guards interchanged between all Chrysler lines, back to the 1949 models, and many cars were retrofitted with them.

An answer to Studebaker's popular "Hill Holder" was MoPar Autostop, introduced in June. With a flick of the finger, the gearshift lever-mounted control switch semi-automatic service brake lock held the car still, releasing automatically when the accelerator pedal was depressed. Autostop was ideal for hilly areas, to prevent backsliding or rolling forward whether sitting at a stop or when parking. Like most MoPar accessories, Autostop could be retrofitted to earlier models and to other Chrysler car lines.

Plymouth's racing era came to an end in 1952. Plymouth managed a third place in the final points standing, behind Hudson and Oldsmobile, respectively. Plymouth managed to score three first-place finishes (as did Oldsmobile, in comparison to Hudson's twenty-seven), in addition to five second-, eight third-, seven fourth- and six fifth-place finishes. Lee Petty continued to campaign a Plymouth, having traded his 1949 coupe for a 1952. Petty's

usual strategy paid off in a 150-mile race at Macon, Georgia, September 7. The race had been led by a Hudson Hornet, which blew its engine on the last lap allowing Petty to slip the little Plymouth into the winners' circle one more time. One week later Petty scored another win in a 250-mile race at Langhorne, Pennsylvania. Plymouths would continue to compete but were finally being outclassed. As the next racing season approached, Lee Petty switched to a V-8 Dodge.

National Production Authority guidelines continued to define both how many cars the industry could build and how they could be equipped. DeSoto, for example, could only build 65 percent of its cars with automatic transmissions! Chrysler's allocation of 936,486 cars for 1952 was down (from 1.2 million cars the year before), a figure Chrysler exceeded by slightly better than 20,000 units. Ford exceeded its allotment of 918,885 by 83,953 cars, while GM was cut to 1,790,85–a target they missed by 9,765. Total industry sales were down a million cars, Plymouth losing 0.6 percent of its market share from 1951.

As the 1952 model year drew to a close, so too did the career of Dan S. Eddins, long-time head of the Plymouth Division. Eddins had jumped General Motors' ship in 1933, becoming Plymouth's general manager late in 1934. His career guiding Plymouth's growth had been long and distinguished, setting all-time sales records in 1936, 1937, and 1950. When he handed over the reigns to J.P. Mansfield, Plymouth Division was as strong as it had ever been and for the time being, at least, it appeared Plymouth's star would continue to rise.

The final P22 Concords, P23S Cambridges, and P23C Cranbrooks came off the line October 3, 1952, twenty-two months and 1,007,662 cars since production had started. At long last, the new model originally planned for 1952 would finally see the light of day–for better or for worse.

1953: Against All Trends

Government restrictions dictated early in 1952 (aimed at conserving steel for the Korean War) nearly kept Plymouth from introducing its all-new 1953 design. Fortunately the war did not escalate, and, as hopes for peace grew, the restrictions were lifted early enough that the planned model year changeover could take place. The year 1953 marked Plymouth's (and DeSoto's) twenty-fifth an-

The club coupe was available in either Cambridge or Cranbrook trim. The example pictured is a Cambridge. Owner: Rick Wright.

Marketplace(Calendar Year 1953)
Chevrolet–24.2 percent
Ford–19.3 percent
Plymouth–10.6 percent

niversary, but the company chose not to mention its silver anniversary when the new cars made their public debut November 20, 1952. Choosing to ignore the silver anniversary may have been made easier by the fact both Buick and Ford were celebrating their fiftieth anniversaries in 1953. For Plymouth, there would not even be a special model to commemorate the occasion.

If K.T. Keller liked the "larger on the inside, smaller on the outside" cars built from 1949 to 1952, the 1953 Plymouth was an even more perfect car for Keller's tastes. Once again, the cars were downsized; overall length was only 1in shorter, despite a 4-1/2in decrease in wheelbase for all body styles, while interior dimensions were increased including greater headroom. Not a single piece of trim, glass, or sheet metal interchanged with 1952 models.

The twenty-fifth anniversary Plymouths were caught in a time warp—at a time when bigger was better, they had grown smaller. As other makes plastered on chrome trim, Plymouth took it off, making it an extra cost option on even the most deluxe models. As other makes entered the horsepower race and introduced V-8 engines, Plymouth's only powerplant was the twenty-year-old valve-in-block 6-cylinder (but then 50 percent of all cars sold in 1953 were sixes). Plymouth was one of only seven makes not to offer power steering, and of the low-priced three, it was the only one not to offer an automatic transmission. While there were some obvious modern updates, including a curved one-piece windshield and rear fenders integral with the body, there were still throwbacks to the old days like the cowl ventilator. For traditionally conservative Plymouth buyers, this was a car with which they could be comfortable. And sales suggested Plymouth was on the right track, as the 1953 models

surpassed by nearly 40,000 units the sales record set just two years earlier.

Plymouths for 1953 were built under the single engineering code of P24. The code letters S and C, which had been used in previous years to indicate standard or deluxe models, were dropped in favor of additional number codes to indicate the model series. Model series were pared to just two, the less expensive cars sold as the Cambridge (P24-1), while the Cranbrook (P24-2) continued as the deluxe line. The short wheelbase Concords were discontinued in favor of a single chassis for all series, a chassis that was 3in longer on the less expensive cars but 4-1/2in shorter on the upscale cars.

Cambridge body styles included a four-door sedan, club (two-door) sedan, business coupe, and two-door Suburban station wagon. The club sedan and business coupe shared the same general body details, the club sedan having a slightly different roofline and rear quarter window divider bar while the business coupe did not. The business coupe deleted the rear seat to make room for a traveling salesman to carry his wares. An optional rear seat could be installed at trade-in time and the car traded off as a regular passenger car. Business coupe buyers could mount the spare tire in either the trunk compartment or against the back wall of the interior.

Cranbrook body styles included a four-door sedan, club coupe (which did not have a quarter window divider bar), a convertible club coupe, the Cranbrook Belvedere two-door hardtop convertible, and the Savoy station wagon.

For the first time Plymouth's assignment of seri-

This well-dressed Cranbrook sedan wears Cello wire wheel hubcaps, a grille guard, fog lamps, window shades, sun visor, and door handle guards—all MoPar-approved accessories.

The Belvedere name was still applied only to the hardtop convertible. Owner: Paul Langewisch.

Kelsey-Hayes offered real, adjustable spoke wire wheels in either painted or chrome-plate finish. GM used the same wheels. Wheels were expensive then and even more so today. *Jim Benjaminson*

al numbers no longer indicated the model series of the car. In years past, for example, Cranbrooks had been assigned one sequence of numbers, with Cambridges a different sequence and Concords a third sequence. (These number sequences had also indicated the plant of manufacture.) Now regardless of the model series, the serial number indicated only the plant in which the vehicle had been built. To compensate for this change, dealers were notified that it would be necessary to include the body code number on all correspondence regarding a car.

"Beautifully balanced body design" are the words Plymouth used to describe the 1953 cars. The cars' silhouettes were lower, at least in corporate eyes, but the overall shortness of the package contributed even more to the square and boxy Keller three-box school of styling. The one-piece windshield had a gentle curve, finally eliminating the center divider bar. The one-piece hood sat lower, providing an even better view of the roadway. Even the traditional Mayflower sailing ship sat lower, directly above a new medallion featuring the Plymouth crest and nameplate. Headlamps sat higher and wider apart, with the parking lamps located directly below at the extreme outer ends of the grille bar, which flowed into a similarly shaped body crease wrapping around the side of the car to form a rub rail contour on the front fender. This rub rail ran back to the leading edge of the front door. A similar rub rail began on the lower rear door flowing across the rear fender to a point just beneath the parabolic-shaped taillight lens. The grille was a simple horizontal bar flowing from the rub rail on one fender to the other. Only the center third of the grille was chrome (if the purchaser had opted for the chrome grille option) while the outer

thirds were painted to match the color of the body. The painted sections of the grille were adorned with two vertical chrome teeth (which detractors said gave the car a "buck-tooth" appearance). Chrome strips on the front fender rub rails and a similar strip on the rear quarter rub rails were optional on all models. It should be noted these cars may have been deliberately designed devoid of chrome trim—when they were on the drawing board government restrictions on copper, nickel, and chrome were still in effect. Regardless, the final result was a "Plain Jane" automobile. "I remember two dealer meetings where the cars drew loud complaints," recalls William Burge, a long-time South Dakota dealer. "One of the meetings was on the 1953 models (the other the 1962). In 1952 we sold a quality car, but in 1953 they cheapened them something terrible. . . ."

Another long-time dealer, C.D. Murray of Colby, Kansas, had even harsher words for the car: "The 1953 Plymouth was a bastard, dusty S.O.B. I had to buy an undercoating machine from a Ford dealer who quit—if you remember [the] '49 Ford was a dusty S.O.B., too—you would've thought Chrysler would've been wise to that. I undercoated every new car as soon as I got them, give it to the customer if I couldn't collect for it."

Rear door cutouts were changed, the upper door swooping back into the "C" pillar to allow easy entry or exit—a feature "doubly appreciated by women and heavier-than-average persons," according to the dealer data book. Outside door handles were changed to a pull type from the traditional twist type handle Plymouth had used since 1928. In back, the rear and side windows were enlarged. The Plymouth nameplate was less prominent, relocated to the lower left hand of the deck lid, directly above the gas filler cap. After riding on the left rear fender since 1936, Plymouth engineers decided to place the gas filler at the rear of the body, just above the rear bumper, a move made to make it easier to fuel the car from either side. A relief valve in the pipe was supposed to prevent gasoline from surging out of the pipe, but the idea worked better on paper than it did in actual practice. Spilled fuel was one of the major owner complaints noted by Floyd Clymer in his road test of the 1953 Plymouths for *Popular Mechanics*.

Despite its otherwise plain appearance, the addition of real wire wheels (in either painted or chrome trim) was a welcome, albeit expensive, addition to the option list. Kelsey-Hayes announced in September 1952 that it would build 50,000 sets of these wheels for both General Motors and Chrysler Corporation at a cost of "about $50 per unit." The per unit price meant one wheel, hence wire wheels were a fairly rare option even when new.

Interior changes included a revised two-toned

instrument panel with an "eyebrow" over the gauge panel to prevent light reflection into the windshield. The gauge panel remained the same as 1951-52. The glove compartment was relocated to the center of the dash, directly below the radio, and all control knobs had a modern square design. Cranbrooks had a mottled-finish floor mat with the Plymouth crest embedded in it, while Cambridge buyers had to settle for a plain mat. Bright trim accents provided the color break line for door trim panels that were two toned in contrasting shades of vinyl plastic (the darker color used at the lower edge of the panel). Color harmonizing plastic window regulator knobs, escutcheons, and cowl vent knobs were used on all models except the Belvedere, Cranbrook convertible, and Savoy wagon, on which they were chrome plated.

Rear-seat passengers in two-door models were treated to a new "E Z Exit" off-center split seat, allowing the driver and center seat passenger to remain in place on two-thirds of the seat, while the right third of the back rest folded forward to allow rear-seat passengers entry or exit.

For years, one of Plymouth's selling features had been the "economy" of removable rear fenders should they need replacement following an accident. Plymouth's new integral rear fenders found the factory backpedaling to explain the change: they were "welded directly to the rear quarter panels, adding to Plymouth's compact, unified look" claimed advertisements. If they should need repair, Plymouth assured the buyer "access to the rear fenders through the luggage compartment makes removal of minor dents and dings simple and economical."

Plymouths for 1953 sat on a fully boxed, four crossmember perimeter frame that was 6in wider than before. The rear axle was moved 4-1/2in ahead of center on the rear springs, with a higher kick-up for the axle, resulting in the frame sitting lower than before, especially over the rear compartment. This allowed a flatter floor and more legroom in the rear seat. Suspension changes included non-parallel control arms on the front suspension to reduce body tilt on outward turns, a front sway bar, and splay-mounted rear springs. Splay mounting was accomplished by moving the rear ends of the springs outward and suspending them under the frame on rubber-insulated shackles. Front ends of the springs were mounted inside the frame on silent block rubber bushings. This, along with a 2in spring width, and longer anchor pins, helped resist twist and sway. Rear springs consisted of only five tapered leaves, grooved for lightness and strength, the ends of the upper leaves separated by interliners of wax-impregnated fabric. Rear shock absorbers were mounted "sea leg," slanting inward toward the center of the car to add to comfort, stability, and safety.

Under the hood sat the same engine as had been used since 1942, a 217ci six now rated at an even 100hp by virtue of a 0.1 increase in compression. At the beginning of the model year, Plymouth offered only two transmission choices, three-speed manual or three-speed manual with overdrive. In his test of the 1953 Plymouth, Floyd Clymer wrote, "One characteristic of Plymouth owners that sets them apart from those with other makes is: They are not too favorably disposed toward automatic transmissions. Plymouth does not feature this, and only 33 percent said they want some form of automatic transmission in their next car." A semi-automatic transmission introduced in April—called Hy-Drive—would have to suffice until a fully automatic transmission arrived in 1954. Clymer's figures

Station wagon sales continued to grow; only two-door wagons were available. Owner: Stan Sides. *Jim Benjaminson*

Aftermarket suppliers offered a number of speed items to bolster 6-cylinder horsepower. Seen here is a Tattersfield finned-aluminum high-compression head. *Jim Benjaminson*

Two-tone paint was proving to be popular. Although it had been available on the 1952 P23 Cranbrook series sedan and club coupe, few cars were seen with the option until 1953. Stainless trim was kept to a minimum even on this top of the line Cranbrook sedan. Owner: Norman Townsend.

weren't far off—by year's end, Hy-Drive would be fitted into one out of every four cars coming off the line.

Hy-Drive, in its simplest form, placed a torque converter—instead of a flywheel—ahead of the standard clutch and transmission. Hy-Drive was a scaled down version of the "Gyro-Torque Drive" used by Dodge. The Hy-Drive torque converter produced an engine torque multiplication of 2.6:1 (the highest in the industry), in combination with an 8-1/2in, twelve-spring, high-pressure clutch with sixteen (rather than ten) splines coupled to a Synchro-silent transmission modified to absorb the added torque. Like all automatics, a neutral safety switch allowed Hy-Drive cars to only be started while in neutral. To get underway it was still necessary to manually shift into high gear, but from that point Hy-Drive eliminated the need for shifting, except under emergency conditions or when shifting into reverse.

The Hy-Drive converter consisted of four major parts: an impeller, turbine, and primary and secondary stators. The converter was a welded, self-contained assembly, although the starter ring could be serviced separately. The Hy-Drive converter received its oil supply from the engine oil pump through passages in an adapter plate and the converter housing. A ball check valve in the converter maintained engine oil pressure at 20lb during low engine speeds providing a constant supply of oil to the converter without surges due to different engine rpms. An internal bypass valve in the oil pump recirculated the oil within the pump instead of allowing returned oil from the converter to return directly to the oil pan. An oil filter bypass valve was located left of the engine block where the engine oil pressure relief valve was located on cars without Hy-Drive.

Because the Hy-Drive converter shared oil with the engine, 11qts (with filter) were required when changing oil. Plymouth recommended only two oil changes per year, one in the spring and one in the fall. Replacement of the Hy-Drive oil filter was recommended every 5,000mi, or more frequently when operated in extremely dusty areas or for short distances in cold weather. When changing oil, the oil pan and torque converter had to be drained separately although the refill was done in the conventional manner.

Hy-Drive cars were specially built in more respects than just the addition of a torque converter. Hy-Drive transmissions were shorter, with no extension at the rear of the case and had heavier gear teeth to carry the additional torque. Hy-Drive gear ratios were different, using 2.37:1 first gear and 1.68:1 second gears. Hy-Drive cars had a larger cooling area radiator (with approximately the same coolant capacity), a different clutch disc, and a longer propeller shaft. Carburetors in Hy-Drive cars were equipped with a dash pot, a longer speedometer cable was required, the rear engine support cross-member was bolted in place, and the clutch linkage was heavier. Even the floor pan of the body was changed to provide increased clearance for the convertor.

Hy-Drive cars were so different that the factory advised dealers "it would not be practical to attempt to install a Hy-Drive unit except in production." Even an item as simple as an engine change called for a special Hy-Drive block.

Record sales kept Plymouth in third place, although Buick continued to make a strong showing in its bid to overtake that position. Lack of sheet steel had kept January production below 2,700 cars per day. New car production in April saw Plymouth building 12,000 cars per week, to Ford's 20,000 and Chevrolet's 27,500 cars. By June production schedules had risen to 3,000 cars per day. Then came July, when Ford began an all out blitz to overtake number-one Chevrolet. Ford simply began overstocking its dealers, dumping huge quantities of unordered cars on them. When the dealers asked how they were to sell the cars, Ford told them it didn't care how—just do it. When dealers complained they were told to either sell the cars, or Ford would find someone else who could. The blitz increased Ford sales to the point where Chevrolet could no longer sit idly by, and it, too, began dumping cars on its dealers. Despite the fact Plymouth's 1953 sales were up 40 percent over 1952, it found itself caught in the middle of the Ford/Chevrolet War—and even had they wanted to, Plymouth lacked the plant capacity to join the war. Additionally, Chrysler's franchise agreement with dealers committed it to build cars only to dealer's orders. All it could do was sit on the sidelines and watch. For Plymouth it would spell a disheartening slip in mar-

The instrument panel used the same gauge layout as the 1951–52 cars. The dash panel was painted rather than wood grain. *Norman Townsend*

For the price of one Kelsey-Hayes real wire wheel, buyers could get a full set of Cello wire wheel hubcaps through their Plymouth parts man. Other makes, including Kaiser, used the Cello cap. *Jim Benjaminson*

ket share the next year. For many of the independents, it simply spelled doom. General Motors, Ford Motor Company, and Chrysler Corporation controlled 88.2 percent of the 1953 market, leaving precious little to be divided among Studebaker, Nash, Packard, Kaiser, and the others.

Plymouth's days of glory on the nation's race tracks had all but come to an end by 1953. Lee Petty and other Plymouth stalwarts had abandoned the 6-cylinder cars for V-8 power, leaving only a winless Dave Terrell to continue campaigning a six. Plymouth's 1953 race standings showed no first-place wins and only one second-place finish. Plymouths did manage to eke out four third-place, three fourth-place and five fifth-place finishes. Plymouth's only victory came from overseas, when a Plymouth captured first place in the Francorchamps Stock Car Race in Belgium, winning its class at 81.2mph.

Plymouth fared better overseas in gas mileage marathons than it did in the U.S., capturing the first four positions in economy trials held in Belgium, taking top honors at 25.3mpg. On the home front, Plymouth only managed a fifth (out of six positions) in the Ninth Mobil Gas Economy Run from Los Angeles to Sun Valley, Idaho. Competing in Class A (low price, standard, and overdrive transmission) a Plymouth Cranbrook recorded fourth best mileage of 22.83mpg, but fifth (at 46.95) in ton/mpg, far behind the winning Ford Mainline six at 27.03mpg and 56.7ton/mpg. The only car in the class scoring lower gas mileage was a Ford Mainline V-8 at 22.52mpg.

Chrysler Corporation Parts Division, better known as MoPar, began offering several interesting accessories during 1953. January saw the introduction of wire wheel covers for all cars equipped with 15in wheels. At $49.75 for a set of four, they were considerably less expensive then the genuine wire wheels built by Kelsey-Hayes. The MoPar wire wheel cover had a plain hubcap, while another factory-approved wire cover featured a Lancer crest, crown, and crossed sword medallion. This cap, made by Cello Wire Wheel of Boston and costing $89.50 per set, fit into the wheel rim and was held in place by the wheel lug nuts. The Cello design was used not only by Plymouth and its sister division DeSoto but by Nash and Kaiser as well.

Another January MoPar offering was a dual tailpipe extension kit for Plymouth (and Dodge). The kit consisted of a "Y" pipe and two chrome-plated exhaust extensions to give the illusion of a V-8-powered car with dual exhausts. February saw the release of lower sill protective molding for all cars except the convertible. Outside companies capitalized on the lack of chrome trim on the 1953 Plymouth, offering front and rear rub rail moldings for the Cambridge and a continuous door finish molding for both Cambridge and Cranbrook sedans. Ironically these same trim pieces would be standard equipment on 1954 Belvederes!

Customized cars were all the rage, so it was only natural that Plymouth attempted to cash in on the craze by offering a factory Continental spare tire carrier for all models except the Suburban. Two kits were offered depending on whether the car was fitted with wire wheels or not. The rear mounting of the spare tire allowed the full trunk space to be utilized. Several aftermarket suppliers also offered continental kits for the Plymouth, including Hudelson-Whitebone, the largest maker of continental kits. Newhouse Automotive, a popular aftermarket

Plymouth preferred to call its two-door models Club Sedans. A business coupe with a slightly different roofline was also available. Owner: Gerald Konkol.

parts supplier, offered a fake "full Continental" for $135 (the spare tire remained in the trunk) or a bustle-back Continental (which bolted to the deck lid and gave a false impression of a rear-carried spare tire) for $34.95.

April saw the addition of factory-designed fender skirts, while August brought the most outrageous accessory in the form of dual fender-mounted trumpet style air horns. Externally mounted chrome horns had last appeared on the 1936 Plymouths, mounted by special brackets under the headlamps. For 1953 Plymouth offered four horn kits, including one set with 18in and 23in trumpets to be mounted on either front fender, a single black painted coiled horn for under-hood mounting, or a choice of side-by-side trumpets on a single base for fender mount-

ing, one set with 10-1/2in and 13in trumpets, the other with 12in and 18in trumpets. A 5x9in heavy steel air tank, 70lb compressor, and power unit were mounted under the hood, with the control switch mounted on the gearshift lever. As conservative as Plymouth was in its 1953 styling, it is hard to believe that such an outlandish accessory was offered. Plymouth may not have been able to out run all the cars on the road, but they could at least blast their way through traffic.

Although the horsepower race was still a few years off, Plymouth was definitely losing among the low-priced three, Chevrolet boasting 115hp to the Ford V-8's 110. Even the Ford six, at 101hp, bettered the 100hp Plymouth. Aftermarket manufacturers came to the rescue for those willing to spend extra money to add needed horsepower to the now rather anemic Plymouth six. Edmunds offered a dual intake manifold for all Plymouth sixes back to 1937 for $41.25 along with a high compression head for $52.50, a rather substantial outlay for a few more horsepower. Weiand, Tattersfield, and Offenhauser all offered dual intake manifolds and Weiand a finned aluminum head for the Plymouth six. Another popular hop up trick was "splitting" the manifold to create dual exhausts.

According to Floyd Clymer's polling of 1953 Plymouth owners for *Popular Mechanics*, 75 percent indicated they had owned a Plymouth previously, with 18 percent claiming to have owned five or more. Forty-seven percent of owners rated their cars as excellent, while 40 percent rated the car as good. Only 1 percent gave the car a poor rating. When asked their likes about the car, 97 percent

Tattersfield offered a dual carbur manifold. While many were content to "split" the regular manifold, Fenton and other manufacturers offered a dual outlet manifold. *Jim Benjaminson*

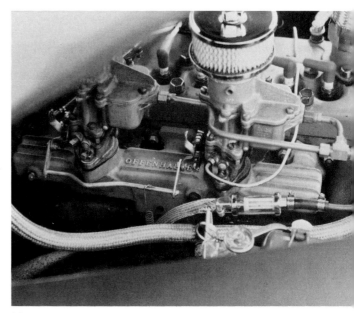

Offenhauser also made a dual carb manifold for the Plymouth six. Any of these speed-related items are extremely rare today. *Jim Benjaminson*

commented on the excellent forward visibility. Only 28 percent liked the location of the gas filler. Major complaints centered on the gas filler pipe and poor workmanship, including paint and chrome work. Sixty-four percent said they would buy another Plymouth, with just 4 percent saying they would not.

As the final P24 Plymouths rolled off the line September 18, 1953, Plymouth looked back on its best year ever. As the year drew to a close, Chrysler Corporation invested $35 million to purchase the Briggs Manufacturing Company. The acquisition of Briggs, which supplied bodies not only to Chrysler but to Packard and others, added twelve plants and 6.5 million square feet of floor space to the already vast Chrysler holdings. Chrysler's new Indianapolis transmission plant came on-line supplying Power-Flite automatics, and both Evansville and San Leandro assembly plants each built their 1 millionth car. A March price cut of about $100 per car had helped Plymouth maintain its traditional third place by a substantial margin over Buick. Then came 1954 . . .

1954: Disaster Strikes

Plymouth debuted its 1954 models October 15, 1953, with a slightly warmed-over redesign and high hopes for another successful year–after all, the 1953 Plymouth had set an all-time record for new car sales. Besides, the Korean War was history, government restrictions had been lifted, the economy was solid, and people had money to spend, so there was little reason not to be optimistic. Content with a mild restyle for 1954–"refreshing newness" Plymouth called it–only a new grille and taillamps plus the addition of body side chrome (which had been offered by outside suppliers for 1953) served to differentiate the 1954 Plymouth from the 1953.

Plymouth once again offered three distinct series, pirating the model names from body styles of the past. At the top of the line was the Belvedere (engineering code P25-3), which previously had been the name of Plymouth's two-door hardtop convertible. The Belvedere line consisted of a four-door sedan, a sport coupe (formerly the Belvedere hardtop convertible), a convertible coupe, and the two-door all-metal Suburban station wagon.

Next in line was the Savoy series (coded P25-2), a name formerly reserved for the deluxe Suburban station wagon. Savoys came in four-door

sedan, club sedan, or club coupe body styles. At the bottom of the pricing ladder sat the Plaza series, code P25-1. Plazas could be had in four-door sedan, club sedan, business coupe, or Suburban station wagon format.

Restyling the front grille work did away with 1953's buck-toothed look. The main grille bar was chromed across its width, extended across the entire forefront of the car, and acted as a beveled cap for the rub rail contour line on the front fender. In the center of the grille bar Plymouth was spelled out in red block letters against a gold plastic background. Above the nameplate and centered on the sloping face of the hood was a new hood medallion bearing a chrome Plymouth crest on color with the Mayflower floating proudly on stylized waves. The

<hr>

Marketplace(Calendar Year 1954)
Chevrolet–25.6 percent
Ford–25.1 percent
Plymouth–7.2 percent

<hr>

Second Chance—The Secret Life of the 1953–54 Plymouth as a Chrysler

Despite its poor showing in U.S. sales, the 1953-54 body would remain in production in Australia until early 1964. The 1955 Plymouths, while an outstanding success in the United States, were a dismal flop in the Land Down Under. Twenty V-8 Belvederes were imported, but sales were so slow no more cars were brought over. In an attempt to build an "all-Australian" car like General Motors' Australian-built Holden and Australian-built Fords, Chrysler-Australia secured the body dies and began building one line of cars, under the Chrysler Royal nameplate, replacing the previous Plymouth, Dodge, and DeSoto models.

Introduced in 1957, the Royal was available as a four-door sedan only, engineering coded AP1 (sources argue whether AP stood for Australian Plymouth or Australian Production). The Royal—at around £2,000 Australian—was an expensive car. Later the Royal four door was joined by the Plainsman station wagon and still later by the Wayfarer coupe-utility. Updated versions known as the AP2 and AP3 were built until the Royal was phased out of production; the last cars sold early in 1964. Utilizing the 1953 American body, Chrysler Australia added front and rear fenders from the U.S.version 1956 Plymouth, complete down to the 1956 taillights. The AP2 fitted a second fin atop the 1956 style fin and adapted a 1957 DeSoto-style front bumper and grill. Side trim was a clone of the U.S. DeSoto Fireflite.

Early cars were powered by a 230ci engine when mated with a standard transmission and a 250ci six when equipped with the two-speed Power-Flite automatic. Later cars got V-8 power (based on the Canadian 313ci engine) and TorqueFlite three-speed automatic. Standard equipment included vinyl upholstery, carpeting, radio, heater-defroster, and tinted glass in all windows. Options included power brakes and power steering, as well as overdrive in addition to the automatics. During its seven-year production run in Australia, slightly more than 13,000 1953 Plymouth-bodied Chrysler Royals were built.

Several aftermarket manufacturers, as well as MoPar parts, offered continental kits for the 1954 Plymouth. Factory kits can be identified by the way the tire moves to the side for access to the trunk. Owner: Viril Layton. *Jim Benjaminson*

outer arms of the medallion pointed outward to the newly designed headlamps set inside extended bezels on Belvedere and Savoy models. The Mayflower sailing ship was again redesigned, a "stylized ship in gleaming chrome, streamlined and properly positioned to enhance the overall feeling of sleekness."

Belvederes were treated to a full-length chrome sill molding and full-length side moldings running from the front fender rub rail back to the rear fender stone shield, then dropping slightly to extend rearward on the rear fender rub rail. On all models a chrome belt molding running beneath the windows and above the deck lid provided the color break line for two-tone paint combinations. Belvederes were also graced with a chrome rear fender molding, which gave just the slightest hint of a fin and added the illusion of extra length to the car.

Exterior basket-weave trim beneath the window sills was added later in 1954 year to dress up the convertible. The Belvedere name, originally applied to just the hardtop convertible was extended to an entire line of body styles including this convertible. Owner: Laurence Frank.

The 1954 Plymouth was longer than its 1953 sibling by 3-5/8in–accomplished by moving the bumpers outward. The public did not share Plymouth's enthusiasm for cars that were "bigger on the inside, but smaller on the outside." This subtle change of bumper position suggests that Plymouth was responding to dealer complaints that the cars were just too stubby and looked cheap. Plymouth referred to the bumper move as "not enough to affect Plymouth's compactness–[but] does strongly reinforce the lengthening effect of the new, swift-flowing chrome lines."

Styling changes at the rear of the car were evolutionary, rather than revolutionary. A new deck lid handle, with integrated push-button lock and latch, highlighted the only deck lid change. Cars fitted with Hy-Drive or overdrive had a chrome script on the lower right corner of the deck lid, with the word "Plymouth" in the lower left corner of the lid as before. With the addition of PowerFlite later in the year, a small stick-on nameplate signifying that transmission was placed directly above the deck lid lift. Taillamps and back-up lamps were united in distinctive chrome housings, while redesigned bumper overriders contained the lights for the rear license plate. Belvedere Sport Coupes now boasted a one-piece rear window.

"It is fitting indeed that these dashing–almost daring–1954 Plymouths should be introduced to the public in the autumn–most brilliant season of the year," read the dealer data book, "for in these new cars it's color that packs the new styling with extra impact–color that enlivens the car from rubber to roof. Plymouths take their cue from the rainbow." Belvedere buyers had the choice of several two-tone combinations, each utilizing either San Leandro Ivory or black for the color of the top, while Suburban purchasers could order two tones with the top in San Mateo Wheat.

Plymouth interiors took on a new look as the familiar pin stripes were discarded. In Belvedere models, all interior hues matched those found on the exterior. Seats in the four-door and sport coupe were finished in damasklike, man-made patterned fabrics in blue, gold, red, or green to match the outer body color. Bolsters were finished in pleated, soft, Doeskin vinyl in ivory or black, to match the car's roof color. Door trim panels carried the same two tones; an insert of patterned vinyl matching the seat fabric was enclosed above and below trim panels of solid, upholstery-color vinyl. Slender, chrome moldings highlighted the lines of separation. A spear-like, fluted band of chrome swept forward from the rear armrest to intersect both colors. The front seat base was also highlighted by a fluted band of chrome. Floor coverings were integrated into the picture with genuine wool carpeting in body color (marking Plymouth's first use of carpet on front compartment floors), highlighted by alu-

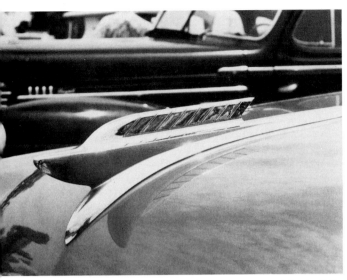

The Mayflower ornament was becoming more stylized all the time. *Jim Benjaminson*

The Plaza Suburban wagon was a "plain Jane" but proved to be a popular vehicle nonetheless. Owner: Dave Kimball.

minum door sill plates. Headliners of finely woven fabric matched the primary body color. Exterior body colors continued on the inside across the top, sides, and bottom of the instrument panel with the instruments and radio set in a long central island, finished in either ivory or black to match the outside top color, or San Mateo Wheat in convertible and Suburban bodies (at the federal government's request, this would be the first year that Civil Defense markings, at 640kc and 1240kc, would appear on radio sets). The top of the instrument panel was painted in a No-Glare finish. Even the three-spoke steering wheel with full horn ring was finished in the body top color.

Belvedere convertible and Suburbans used Woodweave—a wheat-colored vinyl material with a realistic woven reed finish in conjunction with leather-like vinyl in seats and door panels. Woodweave inserts surrounded by a dipped belt line molding were additions to exterior trim on Belvedere convertibles later in the year. Convertible buyers were also given the choice of convertible tops in green or blue in addition to the traditional tan or black.

Savoy interiors were available in three two-tone color combinations: deep and light green, dark and light blue, or brown with beige. The lighter tone was found on the ladder-pattern fabric of the seat cushions and the pleated tufted seatbacks, the contrasting darker tone in the solid color bolsters. The seat pattern carried over to the door panels, bordered above and below in bolster color, with chrome moldings separating the color lines. A fluted chrome band highlighted the front seat base while the deep colors carried over into the instrument panel, garnish moldings, headliner, and the carpet-like rubber floor mats. The instrument panel

island and steering wheel were finished in harmonizing lighter tones.

As the price leader, Plaza buyers found a fabric interior carrying a blue or green pattern on a gray background. This color and pattern was carried over to the door panels that were bordered top and bottom in a darker shade of plain vinyl. The headliner, garnish moldings, instrument panel, and steering wheel blended into the color scheme. In the Plaza Suburban, seats and panels were trimmed with vinyl simulating leather in two-tone combinations of deep blue and light gray or dark and light green.

Plymouth continued the use of a cowl ventilator on all models. Belvedere and Savoy sedans had lockable, manually controlled vent wings on rear doors as well as the front, and Plymouth's famous high geared 2-1/2-turn window risers were retained.

As the production run began, Plymouth retained the same mechanical features as the 1953 models. Wheelbase remained unchanged at 114in for all models. Only one engine was available, with the choice of three-speed manual, three-speed with overdrive, or Hy-Drive semi-automatic transmissions. Plymouth still didn't offer power brakes, but power steering was finally added to the options list.

At $139.75, Plymouth's power steering was not cheap. Unlike many add-on power steering systems, Plymouths version was built as a complete factory unit. The hydraulic pump and oil reservoir were built as part of the generator and mounted on the engine's left side. The system was fairly simple, with a power link replacing the conventional drag link in the steering linkage. Because the power steering was an integral part of the steering linkage, the car could be safely steered when the engine was not running or when the unit was not functioning.

The Savoy four-door sedan proved to be a popular seller. This example has just 48,000 miles. Owner: John McKenry III.

April saw the addition of the PowerFlite automatic transmission to the option list—at long last Plymouth could compete head to head with Chevrolet and Ford. With PowerFlite came a more powerful engine as well, a 110hp 230ci six borrowed from Dodge. (Even at 110hp, Plymouth still trailed Ford by 5hp and a Powerglide-equipped Chevrolet by 15hp.) In addition, Ford had a new overhead valve V-8 to crow about. At $189 PowerFlite was only slightly more than the $146 Hy-Drive option. Like Hy-Drive, PowerFlite was a two speed using essentially the same torque converter. The main difference was that the PowerFlite converter was supplied with oil from a reservoir in the transmission rather than sharing oil from the engine. Integrated with a planetary gear seat, Power-

Flite multiplied engine torque 4.47 times compared to Hy-Drive's 2.6 multiplication. Unlike Hy-Drive, PowerFlite eliminated the need for a clutch pedal. Shifting was normally required only to get underway or to go into reverse. Engine braking could be accomplished by pulling the selector lever into the low range, which locked the transmission in low gear. Unlike many of the GM automatics, which required a shift through all the gears to get into reverse, PowerFlite's quadrant put reverse at the top of the sequence, followed by neutral, drive, and low. As would be common practice for Chrysler automatics, no park position was provided, necessitating the use of the hand brake when parking. Because of the difference in the PowerFlite transmission itself, the parking brake was a special, heavy-duty internal-expanding type rather than the external contracting type used since 1928.

Running changes made build-date identification necessary on PowerFlite transmissions, with each transmission having a date code stenciled on the right front corner of the transmission case. The date code consisted of a letter and two sets of numbers. The letter was an alphabetic code corresponding to the months of the year—the letter "A" signifying January, "B" February and so on. Only the letter "I" was skipped (being replaced by "J" for September) to avoid confusion with the number one. The second set of numbers indicated the day of the month, with the final two letters signifying the year (thus a transmission built on September 14, 1954, would have a code date of J-14-54). By the end of the year PowerFlite would be installed in 61,000 cars. The slightly less expensive Hy-Drive (which would disappear at the end of the model run) was installed in 75,000 cars.

Plymouth again followed its tradition of bor-

Another Plymouth double-ender, this one built from two convertibles, made a great advertising promotion for the Swan Lounge in New Albany, Indiana. Owner: S.C. Hubbach.

Plymouth's top-of-the-line sedan this year was the Belvedere. Buyers had the choice of semi-automatic "Hy-Drive" or fully automatic "PowerFlite." Owner: Darrel Davis.

rowing a larger engine from its sister division Dodge, in offering the 230ci, 110hp engine. Dodge's engine had been in use since 1942 (when Plymouth moved up to the Dodge 217). Over the years the 230's horsepower ratings had fluctuated, from 102 after World War II to 103 during the early 1950s, to 110 for 1954. At 230ci, the venerable old six had reached its "safe" limits as far as its 3-1/4x4-5/8in bore and stroke were concerned. In years past when Plymouth claimed a Dodge engine, Dodge had simply increased its engine size to compensate. Now Dodge would have to be content with sharing the same dimensions—though through the magic of engineering (or an ad writer's pen) Dodge's rated horsepower would always be slightly more than Plymouth's.

Strangely enough Plymouth chose to use the same engineering code, P25, for the larger 230ci engine that it had on the 217. To differentiate between the two, the 230 engine serial number was prefixed by a "diamond" before the code number. Engine numbers also ran in different numerical sequences, the change occurring at engine number P25-243001. In addition, a diamond was cast into the left rear corner of the cylinder head on the larger engines.

Rear axle ratios on all body styles equipped with standard transmission, Hy-Drive, or Power-Flite were the same, using 3.73 gearing. Overdrive cars were the only ones to use a 4.1 rear axle.

Tire size on all body styles was 6.70x15in mounted on 4-1/2x15in safety rim wheels.

Plymouths continued to be the most popular taxi cab choice in America. The taxi package offered commercial duty chassis springs, heavy-duty shocks, heavier gauge springs in seats and seatbacks, a 10in clutch on manual transmission cars (8-1/2in on Hy-Drive and 9-1/4in on overdrive-equipped cars), battery heat shields, and a heavy-duty 125amp-hour battery.

Plymouth managed to score only a fourth place in the 1954 Mobil Gas Economy Run, which was again run between Los Angeles and Sun Valley, Idaho. Averaging 22.44mpg (47.71ton/mpg) the overdrive-equipped Belvedere sedan followed a Studebaker Champion, Ford Mainline 6, and Ford Mainline V-8 (all overdrive equipped) in the standings, besting only a Chevrolet 210. It should be noted that the Mobil Gas Economy Run was driven by professional drivers using every trick in the book to eke out top mileage figures and did not truly represent "real world" driving conditions.

Plymouth launched a campaign in 1972 to find the best 1954 Savoy four door in the country after hearing country singer Johnny Cash comment that the 1954 Plymouth Savoy was the "best car I ever owned." People entering the contest agreed to part with their Savoy in exchange for a new 1972 Gran Coupe. *Chrysler Historical Foundation*

Both *Motor Trend* and *Hop Up & Motor Life* magazines road tested a Hy-Drive-equipped Belvedere sedan in their respective January and March issues with amazingly similar mileage results.

Test	Hop Up & Motor Life	Motor Trend
Mileage, steady 30mph	22.4	22.8
Mileage, steady 45mph	20.7	20.9
Mileage, steady 60mph	16.5	16.0
Mileage, steady 75mph	13.4	N/A
Total mileage-MPG	1,216/16.0	812/15.2
Top speed	86.17	85.96

Performance tests by the two magazines also netted similar readings. *Motor Trend* covered the quarter mile in 22.7sec, *Motor Life* in 22.4. Accelerating from 0–60mph took *Motor Life* drivers 24.5sec to *Motor Trend*'s 24.7sec.

Motor Trend later road tested an overdrive-equipped Belvedere Suburban in its September station wagon issue, recording a 17.3mpg average with a top speed of only 72.1mph.

Winning the contest was Mrs. Ray Hild, a retired 77-year-old school teacher from Tacoma, Washington, who parted with her 14,500-mile car in exchange for a 1973 (rather than 1972) Gran Coupe. James J. Bradley, head of the National Automotive Library section of the Detroit Public Library, was hired to examine each car and determine the winning car, which was then given to Cash. *Chrysler Historical Foundation*

Twenty-six years later Joe Suminski, Paul Curtis, and Jim Fiori of the Plymouth Owners Club road tested a similar Belvedere sedan for the *Plymouth Bulletin*. Borrowing an electric fifth wheel from Chrysler Corporation, the then twenty-six-year-old car, showing just 33,000 miles on the odometer, zipped through the quarter mile in 22.5sec at 66mph. Considerably lower was a 0-60mph time of 18.5sec.

The Joie Chitwood Auto Daredevils switched, briefly, from Ford to 1954 Plymouths in their show (before switching to Chevrolet the next year). The Chitwood shows had evolved from the late Lucky Teter's Hell Drivers, which had used Plymouth exclusively in the late 1930s. After the switch to Chevrolet in 1955, the Chitwood cars bore a take off of Plymouth's old familiar "Look At All Three" slogan reading, "I've tried all three, comparison proves Chevy for me."

Despite its attempts at righting the wrongs committed with the 1953 cars, Plymouth soon found itself in deep trouble in the sales arena. By December 1953, two- and three-day work weeks were common during the holiday season as sales began to tumble. January sales slumped 29 percent below that of the previous year, causing Chrysler President L. L. Colbert to call in 1,700 field men for a full week's "skull session." Plymouth's second shift was eliminated on January 11, idling 2,350 workmen. January 25 saw production schedules cut from 2,100 to just 1,200 cars per day. By early February sales were down 40 percent from 1953, with the factory building sold orders only. The first week of March saw an upsurge in sales, resulting in 2,000 Plymouth plant workers and 5,700 body division workers being called back. This euphoria was short-lived, however, as workers in the Mack Avenue body plant staged a wildcat strike on March 10, idling 8,200 workers including 3,000 at Lynch Road. March 26 saw 900 workers at Evansville laid off. Evansville car output schedules rose forty cars per day on May 3, but on that very same day a week-long labor confrontation was launched in the body division ultimately idling 16,000 workers. Four-day work weeks were the norm in July, when a July 19–23 strike at Dodge Main, which supplied engines and transmissions, held final assembly to just two days per week. When the lines shut down for changeover on August 13, 5,200 of 7,400 additional workmen were laid off. Model year changeover also signaled the end of production at the San Leandro, California, plant (which had been building Plymouths since 1949).

As the final tallies were made, Plymouth discovered that 1954 had been the first year the top line series had not outsold the less expensive models. Belvedere sales had accounted for only 32 percent of total production, a far cry from the record of 86.7 percent Deluxe models sold in 1937. By

1958 the number would slip even further to just 26.5 percent.

Motor Life had predicted that "more than half a million motorists will become owners of 1954 Plymouths during the coming months." When the final tally was in, Plymouth found that it had not only slipped from third place, but had tumbled all the way to fifth. Buick had finally made good on its challenge to take over the number-three spot, and Oldsmobile had followed closely on its coattails to claim fourth. R.L. Polk registrations for 1954 showed Chevrolet in the lead, selling 1,417,453 automobiles to Ford's second place 1,400,440. Buick sales were up 59,000 cars from 1953, placing it third with sales of 513,497 cars. Oldsmobile jumped from seventh to capture fourth place with 407,150 units. Plymouth managed to surpass only Pontiac, which slipped from fifth to sixth.

In one short year, Plymouth had slipped from its all-time production high of 600,447 cars to just 381,078 actual sales production figures showed 463,148 cars built as 1954 models).

Plymouth Dream Cars

One of Chrysler Corporation's downfalls during the early 1950s was its lack of styling. The prewar Chrysler Airflow had been a triumph of engineering, but many considered it ugly, and it didn't sell. The economy and the car's relatively high price had just as much to do with buyers rejecting it, but Chrysler's reaction was to retreat into a shell from which it would not emerge for decades. General Motors proved that styling could sell cars, but it wasn't until 1955 that Chrysler finally answered the challenge. By 1957, Chrysler had wrestled the styling crown away from GM.

Much blame has been laid on Chrysler boss K.T. Keller who demanded "smaller on the outside, bigger on the inside, with room to wear your hat in the car" styling. Unfortunately, Keller had failed to notice that most of the nation now went bareheaded. Yet it was Keller who saw the need to move forward, and it was Keller who hired Virgil Exner away from Studebaker to revitalize a moribund product line.

Detroit had discovered that there was considerable interest in "dream car" design proposals—so much so that GM took their cars on tour, staging elaborate "Motoramas" around the country. Not to be outdone, Ford and Chrysler began displaying their dream cars as well. From 1950 to 1959, Chrysler displayed a string of two dozen cars, all but one of which were fully functional. Most were built in Italy to Chrysler designs.

Italian coachbuilder Pinin Farina was looking for business after WWII, so he built a design proposal on a 1950 Plymouth chassis. This car never came stateside, however, and no photos are known to exist. The Ghia coachbuilding works of Torino, Italy, was also struggling in the postwar period. Mario Boano and Luigi Segre approached Chrysler Export Vice-President C.B. Thomas and offered to build a show car for just $10,000. Thomas, recognizing a bargain, had them proceed with what became the Plymouth XX-500, a four-door sedan on the 1950 P20 118-1/2in chassis. The result was a car looking much like the P19 fastback sedan with two additional doors and an Italian accent.

From these modest beginnings, a string of Ghia-built show cars followed, culminating with the Turbine Specials during the 1960s. Most dream cars

The first Plymouth dream car was this Ghia-bodied XX-500 built on a 118-1/2in P23 chassis. *Andrew G. Weimann II*

bore the Chrysler name, with the odd Dodge or DeSoto tossed in for good measure. As Plymouth's sales fortunes plummeted, two dream cars were assigned Plymouth nameplates.

The first of these was an ungainly looking two-passenger roadster called the Belmont. Unlike the other dream cars, this one was designed and built by Briggs Body (soon to be purchased by Chrysler). The other was a rakish sport coupe called the Explorer.

The Belmont made its public debut at the Chicago Auto Show and no doubt caused more than a few hearts to skip a beat. Resplendent in Azure Blue, the topless, V-8-powered, fiberglass-bodied model gave a glimmer of hope to Plymouth dealers—some predicted this would be Plymouth's answer to the Corvette and Thunderbird.

Although officially tagged a Plymouth, Chrysler described the Belmont as a "styling experiment on a 1954 Dodge chassis." While Plymouth and the small Dodge shared the same 114in wheelbase chassis, only Dodge offered a V-8. Plymouth's first V-8 wasn't

scheduled to appear until 1955 in a model coded the P27 series. Although credited to Dodge, the V-8 in the Belmont carries serial number P27-1014—the fourteenth Plymouth V-8 built! Why this fact was never made public is a secret remaining with Chrysler.

With an overall length of 191-1/2in, the Belmont was not a small car. Overall width was slightly more than 73in with a height of 49.3in. Among the car's unusual features was a radio with power antennae controls located in the center armrest, a removable cloth top, and a spare tire carried in a separate behind-seat compartment.

The Belmont's styling was clean, but soon became dated. *Motor Trend* pictured the car in its May 1954 issue but one year later discounted rumors Plymouth would build it as the design was "too old to consider for production."

The Belmont managed to escape the crusher and surfaced in Oregon in 1988. Its owner, Don Heckler, had purchased it in 1968 when the previous owner had tired of all the attention the Belmont drew

The Belmont roadster was designed and built by Briggs of reinforced fiberglass. Never seriously considered for production, the sporty two door gave Ply- mouth dealers a glimpse of hope during an otherwise bad year. *Chrysler Historical Foundation*

The Belmont's interior shows the down-to-business instrument panel—the only production item was the steering wheel. Under the hood was an early Plymouth V-8. *Chrysler Historical Foundation*

Plymouth's exciting Explorer coupe was designed and built by Ghia. Many of its styling cues ended up on Volkswagen's Karmann-Ghia sport coupe. Power was provided by a 6-cylinder with Hy-Drive. *Chrysler Historical Foundation*

whenever it was driven. Little is known of the car's early history once it departed Chrysler. It did make a dealer tour in Southern California and appeared in the 1956 movie *Bundle of Joy* starring Eddie Fisher and Debbie Reynolds; it is also thought to have been used in the 1957 movie *Mister Cory* starring Tony Curtis.

The restored (but incorrectly painted red) Belmont now resides in the Blackhawk Collection in California and is on display with other Chrysler dream cars of the era.

The second of the 1954 dream cars was the Explorer coupe. Designed and built by Ghia on a 114in wheelbase chassis, the car debuted in the May 1954 *Motor Trend*. Despite its racy good looks, the Explorer was powered by the lowly 110hp 230ci 6-cylinder engine coupled to a Hy-Drive transmission.

The Explorer received metallic green paint and the bucket seat interior was covered with white leather. The car also featured fitted luggage behind the seats and an unusual retractable radio tuner control concealed by a movable instrument panel section. The Explorer was 76.9in wide, 54.4in tall, and, at 185.2in, nearly 6in shorter than the Belmont.

Like the Belmont, the Explorer is now part of a private collection in the U.S.. Along the line the Explorer has undergone tremendous changes, most obviously in the grille—gone are the open vertical bars replaced by a rather ugly Jaguar-looking grille. The front bumper was changed from a two-piece affair to a single bar. Even the windshield wipers have been changed, the originals tracked right and left, but now both track in the same direction.

The Explorer—with an "updated engine"—was offered for sale in the March 1990 issue of *Hemmings Motor News* with an asking price of $95,000. Its whereabouts are unknown at this time.

Plymouth's next show car took a different twist—it was a station wagon. Unlike many of the more impractical show cars, most of the unique items on this one found their way into production.

Designed by Dave Scott, the "Plainsman" started life as a "coupe de ville"-type town car. At Exner's suggestion, Scott modified the design to create a station wagon (wagons were becoming big business at Chrysler). First sketched in February 1954, the order to begin construction was given to Ghia in October 1954.

When the car was unloaded from its shipping crate in Detroit on December 5, 1955, and placed on wheels for the first time, the lead-laden body sank under its own weight. A heavier Chrysler New Yorker suspension was called upon to cure the problem. Powered by a 260ci V-8 the 4,900lb car was thoroughly underpowered.

Displayed first at the Chrysler Building in New York City and later at the seventy-fifth anniversary celebration of the J.L. Hudson Department Store in Detroit, many of the Plainsman's innovations found their way into production including the rear-facing third seat, spare tire mounted in the right rear quarter panel, and power-operated tailgate window.

After its show career, the Plainsman was shipped to a dealer in Havana, Cuba. Following a harrowing escape from the Castro regime, the Plainsman saw use in Mexico, Australia (where it

The rear view of Explorer was just as exciting as the rest of the car. *Chrysler Historical Foundation*

The Explorer's interior featured fitted luggage behind the seats and radio controls in the center console.
Chrysler Historical Foundation

was converted by law to right-hand drive), and Japan before wandering back to the U.S. Today the car is part of the Bortz Dream Car Collection.

The last of the Plymouth dream cars, the Cabana, made its appearance in 1958. Like the Plains-man, the Cabana was a station wagon built on a 124in wheelbase. Unlike Plymouth's other dream cars, it was only a body mockup on a rolling chassis and not a running automobile.

The last of the operable Plymouth dream cars was the 1956 Plainsman station wagon. Many of its styling innovations found their way into regular wagon production.

Chapter 4

1955–1956: Fighting to Regain Third Place

1955: A Complete Turnaround

Had Rip Van Winkle fallen asleep in a Plymouth dealer's showroom in August 1954 as the last of the P25 series Plymouths were still on the showroom floors and awakened on November 17 to see the new 1955 models, he would have been easily convinced that he had truly slept for twenty years. What sat on the showroom floor was, in the words of *Plymouth Bulletin* editor Lanny Knutson, "A Plymouth like none other." Plymouth called it "Startling New"–and rightfully so. *Popular Science* asked, "Do you think old maids will keep buying them?" referring to Plymouth's stodgy image. If ever an automobile company had come full circle in its thinking, the 1955 Plymouth was proof of the turnaround. It was truly a car "For The Young in Heart."

For those who could resist change, there was still a venerable old flathead six with three-speed manual transmission and no-frills models to choose from. For those who wanted change there was much for which to rejoice. In addition to the new "Forward Look" design, there was new V-8 power, air conditioning, power windows, and even power seats.

Marketplace(Calendar Year 1955)
    Chevrolet–23 percent
    Ford–22.3 percent
    Plymouth–9.4 percent

Belvederes used the area beneath stainless trim as the color break in two-tone combinations. Convertible buyers had the choice of four roof colors. Owner: Paul Mitchell.

Chevrolet and Ford also introduced all new models for 1955, the new Chevys making their appearance October 28. Ford's November 12 show date put it on the streets five days ahead of Plymouth. Like Plymouth, Chevrolet's models were revolutionary new cars, also introducing V-8 power for the first time since 1918 while Ford's "Y" block V-8 was in its second year. Whether anyone realized it at the time or not, the horsepower race had just launched from the starting gate. Neither Plymouth nor Chevrolet published horsepower figures for their V-8s in early sales catalogs, but as those figures started to appear, jockeying for the highest rating began.

Jeff Godshall, in the April 1982 issue of *Special Interest Autos,* reflected, "It's hard to say which was more important, the new styling or the new V-8." Without a doubt both revealed the most complete model changeover in Plymouth's history. The 1955 Plymouths were the first cars in which Virgil Exner and his design teams were able to start from a clean sheet of paper. The "Hy-Style" 1954 Plymouth, while a vast improvement over the spartan 1953, had largely relied on ornamentation. The 1955, as Exner noted in *Floyd Clymer's Catalog of 1955,* " . . . is based on the premise that styling must first be conceived as a unity. Ornamentation is then used to accentuate existing highlights rather than to create new ones."

From the outset Exner's designers had been instructed to "correlate form and function in every step," designing a car with motion as its basic styling theme. The result was a design Plymouth crowed "could well become a classic." From the outset, everything was done to make the car look long and low. Roof lines were lowered by 1.35in and the wheelbase increased an inch to 115in. But it was the addition of 10.3in to the overall length of the car that was most noticeable. Front tread was increased by 2.56in, making it the same as the rear tread. The sharply canted front fenders nosed into the air, sweeping in a clean line to the rear of the car where the "fin-like" rear fenders canted toward the rear bumper, all adding to the illusion of greater length. The grille was a simple, single bar as before, only much bolder, rising above the bumper at the extreme ends of the grille cavity, forming a box over the park lamp lens before streaking across the width of the car to join a ribbed center section. Even the hood edge was trimmed in chrome. A massive bumper with a slight prow in the center swept from wheel opening to wheel opening aiding the illusion of extreme length. Like many Plymouths before, the bumper had no protected provision for a front license plate. The deeply hooded headlamps sat in a chromed recess on all models except the Plaza. On top of the hood sat an abstract swept-back fin ornament that was passed off as a sailing ship and below that, on the peak of the hood, sat either of two new ornaments–one with the number eight centered in the valley of a V, with "Plymouth" vee'd at the bottom; the other a horizontal spear, with "Plymouth" in a straight line, signifying 6-cylinder power.

The same design theme was carried over to the car's rear, the taillamps hooded by the cant of the rear fenders, vertical taillamp lenses sitting over round back-up light lenses on all models–even the stripped Plaza. The catch was there were no bulbs behind the lenses, unless the dealer checked the correct box on the order blank. The deck lid sat rather high, the lower lip matching a crease in the body sides, level with the bottom of the taillamp lens, creating a coved area beneath the deck lid and rear bumper. Original designs called for the cove to be painted black, a move that was squelched by the time the car had gotten into production. It wasn't long before custom accessory houses began offering a $17.95 "Sportsation" rear grille featuring a square "egg-crate" pattern for all models except the wagons. Deck lid ornamentation included the 6-cylinder or V-8 designations as used on the hood, in addition to "PowerFlite" or "Overdrive" emblems on the lower right corner of the lid.

Roof lines were accented by a wrap-around "full-view" windshield that curved up into the roof and around the car's side. Unlike many cars that left passengers to contend with a dog-leg, Plymouth's version relied on a rearward slanting A pil-

A deck lid emblem of an "8" inside a "V" indicated which engine was installed in this car. The emblem on 6-cylinder cars was flat. The license plate tells the world what styling the car carries. Owner: John Mitchum.

A new body style for 1956 was the Belvedere Sport Sedan four-door hardtop. A two-piece rear window folded together to give an open-air look. Owner: Larry Janecke. *Jim Benjaminson*

lar leaving an unobstructed door opening. The much maligned gas filler pipe problem of 1953–54 was solved by moving the filler door to the right side of the car, a curious location considering it put

The Savoy was spartan in regular trim. Two-tone cars had a contrasting roof color only. Note the plain "dog dish" hubcaps.

the gas filler pipe on the opposite side of the car when pulling into the local service station.

With the introduction of V-8 power, Plymouth found it necessary to use two model designations; 6-cylinder cars were coded P26, V-8 cars P27. The three model names used in 1954 were carried over, with a corresponding number code added to the engineering code. Six-cylinder Plazas were P26-1, while a V-8 Plaza was a P27-1. For reasons unknown, the Belvedere (still the top of the line) became either a P26-2 or P27-2, while the middle Savoy series became the P26-3 or P27-3.

Plazas were sold in five body styles, including a 6-cylinder-only business coupe (which still lacked a back seat and roll-down rear windows), a two-door club sedan, four-door sedan, two-door station wagon, and, for the first time, four-door station wagon. Savoys could be had in just two body styles, either club sedan or four-door sedan, while the Belvedere offered club sedan, four-door sedan, sport coupe, convertible coupe (which mandated a V-8 engine), and a four-door station wagon.

Identification of the various models was simple if you knew your body side trims. The bottom line

Plaza entered the model year with no side trim whatsoever, though by mid-year it would gain the Savoy chrome spear that ran from the front fender to the trailing edge of the front door. A two-tone Savoy had a narrower strip running forward from above the rear fender crease to the middle of the front door, then curving downward to the rocker panel. This trim, too, would be offered mid-year on the Plaza. Full dress trim for Belvedere and Savoy club sedans, four-door Suburbans, and four-door sedans consisted of exterior windshield visor trim, front door trim, a lower quarter panel medallion, and an extra-wide drip molding. Full dress trim for Belvedere sport coupes consisted of the windshield visor trim and extra wide drip moldings, in addition to the regular trim consisting of a fender-door spear like the Savoy, a chrome molding running forward from the taillamp and sweeping up (rather than down as on the Savoy) to join the door trim near the center of the door. A third trim strip angled from the front edge of the door, down from the fender strip to the rocker panel molding. Plaza two-tone paint saw the roof, but not upper door jambs, painted a contrasting color. Belvederes were commonly painted with the roof and lower body from the front doors back in matching color, with the hood, trunk, upper body, and front fenders in contrast.

Aftermarket manufacturers began offering various trim packages for the Plaza and Savoy models. The same company that offered the "Sportsation" rear grille package offered not only a Belvedere-style trim package (the angles were much sharper than original MoPar trim) but a Dodge Lancer-style trim. The Lancer trim began at the base of the windshield post, angled back across the doors where it swooped up from a "Darrin Dip" (named

for a design cue used by Howard Darrin on some Packard models) to run back across the rear quarter of the car, coming to a stop even with the top of the taillamp. At under $20, the trim packages weren't overly expensive but how popular they proved to be is another matter. Not to be outdone, MoPar Parts Division released their own "Sportone" molding packages, ranging in price from $19 to $33, for Plaza, Savoy, and Belvedere four-door sedans and club coupes.

Interiors were as restyled as the exterior. Getting into the car was a matter of pushing a button on the door handle–Plymouth's first, and last (until 1962), push-button door handles. Once inside, the driver was greeted by a "Flight Deck" instrument panel. Immediately to the left of the steering wheel sat a large round speedometer, flanked on the right by smaller amp and gas gauges. In the name of symmetry, and much cursed by owners, was the placement of the temperature and oil pressure gauges in front of the right seat passenger. Dividing the two instrument groups was provision for a radio above the center-mounted glove compartment. Matching the size of the speedometer on the passenger side of the car was the radio speaker grille. The large speedometer dial on early cars reflected into the windshield and windows, a change remedied early in December by painting the outer edge of the speedometer housing and inner rim of the bezel flat black. Instruments were indirectly lighted (a Plymouth feature since 1928). The light switch and heater controls were located to the left of the speedometer, with the windshield wiper knob and the shift lever, on automatic equipped cars, located to the right of the steering column. "Flite Control" shifting may have been a novel idea, but it raised many eyebrows–the shift control lever

Symmetrical design placed the oil and temperature gauges in front of the passenger. *Merv Afflerbach*

Three-tone interior trim of the Belvedere convertible. *Merv Afflerbach*

stuck right out of the dash! "It puts PowerFlite transmission range selection in a class with such simple operations as turning on the lights," read the brochures. Flite Control's gated shift pattern allowed shifting by feel, and to soothe safety concerns, the protruding lever was designed to snap off with as little as 10lb of pressure. Flite Control lasted just one year, replaced by Chrysler's famous–and equally controversial–push buttons for 1956. Instrument panels were painted to match the seat upholstery (the tops finished in no-glare scotch grain) with the center island matching the seat bolsters.

Once again, all interior trim was color-coordinated to the exterior. Belvedere interiors were, of course, more luxurious than Savoy or Plaza. Black interiors featured "Black Magic" Boucle with an interwoven silver Lurex thread; upholstery in other colors featured a "Ship & Shield" tapestry-like Jacquard cloth, again highlighted with silver Lurex threads, the Plymouth Mayflower embedded throughout the cloth. Savoy buyers were given four choices of interior trim, Plaza buyers three.

Fresh air was still drawn into the interior of the car from a cowl-mounted ventilator. Plymouth also continued to offer electric windshield wipers as standard equipment (with an optional, foot-operated "Jiffy Jet" windshield washer) along with optional "Solar Tint" glass. Seats were built with forty-four coil springs and eleven jack springs, and all two-door models fitted with forward-folding seatbacks divided in a one-thirds, two-thirds configuration. Newly available were several dealer- or owner-installed seat belt packages.

A major improvement with the 1955 models was the switch to suspended brake and clutch ped-

als, eliminating the drafty through-the-floor-type pedals used since 1928. The longer sheet metal boosted trunk space to 33.8cu-ft (up 3cu-ft from 1954), with a counter-balanced deck lid held in the open position by parallel torsion springs. Spare tires were mounted at an angle along the right trunk well, concealing the gas filler pipe that was housed within its own compartment to eliminate gas fumes from entering the car through the trunk.

The new body rode a longer, boxed frame fitted with two additional body mounts, located both inside and outside of the frame rails. Front suspension changes included non-parallel "A" arms with Oriflow shock absorbers mounted inside the coil springs. Splay-mounted rear springs were widened to 2.5in with four leaves on sedans (six on wagons) and Oriflow shocks mounted "sea leg" fashion to prevent side sway. As had been Plymouth's practice since the late 1930s, spring leaves were tapered for quiet operation. Standard equipment on all models was a one-piece, spring steel torsion-type sway eliminator bar. V-8-equipped cars introduced Plymouth buyers to a new type of steering using an idler arm-type linkage with equal length tie rods. Unlike most of its competition, Plymouth continued to build cars with Safety Rim wheels, now fitted with tubeless tires.

Reflecting the need for more stopping power, V-8 sedans were fitted with 11in brakes up front, and 10in brakes out back. Six-cylinder cars featured 10in brakes all around, while V-8 station wagons wore 11in brakes on all corners. As had been its practice, front brakes were serviced by two-wheel cylinders. With the switch to suspended pedals, the master cylinder was moved to the firewall. Parking brakes continued to be mounted on the driveshaft.

Despite its "coming of age" Plymouth still clung to a few remnants of its past. Electrics were still 6-volt, now protected by three sets of circuit breakers. Bull's-eye headlamps continued to be used.

For fleet buyers and those glued to tradition, the PowerFlow six remained available, now pumping out 117hp from 230ci. The six could be coupled to any of Plymouth's three transmissions, including PowerFlite, overdrive, or standard three speed. At 30mph in high gear, the old six turned 2790rpm when equipped with either PowerFlite or the standard transmission; overdrive equipped cars employed a 4.1 axle ratio and dropped this figure to 2147rpm. Both the V-8 and six continued to be mounted using Plymouth's famous Floating Power three-point engine mount.

Biggest news of the year was, of course, the "new" V-8 engine. The engine was not really new and was supplied to Plymouth by Dodge division until a new engine foundry could be completed to supply Plymouth with its own engines. The Dodge V-8, introduced in its "B" series of light-duty trucks,

At long last Plymouth could offer buyers a V-8 in two displacements. *Merv Afflerbach*

Savoy Club Sedan with optional Sportone trim made for an attractive two-color break. Owner: Ray Splinter.

delivered 145hp from a displacement of 241ci. Although a Plymouth V-8 had been rumored for several years, it had been held up by the Korean War (as were V-8 engines for Dodge and DeSoto) and Plymouth's own lack of manufacturing capabilities. Plymouth's first true V-8 would not appear until 1956, and then only slightly changed from the Dodge version.

At first the Plymouth V-8 was offered in two displacements—a 241ci rated at 157hp with a bore and stroke of 3.44x3.25in and a 167hp, 260ci engine with a larger bore of 3.563in. Both engines featured a compression ratio of 7.6:1. Shortly after introduction, a four barrel 177hp version of the 260 hit the streets. Maximum torque was achieved at 2400rpm on all engines, the 241 pumping out 217lb-ft and the 260 claiming 231lb-ft whether two- or four-barrel-equipped. Called the Hy-Fire V-8, the Plymouth version differed from other corporate V-8s in that the engine was not a "Hemi."

The Hemi, which would go on to fame and glory both on the drag strip and race tracks during the late 1960s, was, despite its achievements, an extremely expensive engine to build. The Hy-Fire engine achieved some of the Hemi's free-breathing characteristics by placing intake and exhaust valves diagonally opposite each other in the combustion chamber. This provided better breathing while not

restricting valve size as was the case in some other small block engine designs. The design not only allowed adequate "breathing" on the intake cycle but allowed the exhaust valve to open further into the

Unlike the Belvedere convertible, the Belvedere Sport Coupe could be had with 6-cylinder power. This car sports Cello wire-wheel hubcaps and fender skirts, both factory accessories. Owner: Willard Stein.

89

Cars with automatic transmissions had the shift lever mounted through the dash. In the event of a crash, as little as 10lb of pressure would snap the lever. *Chrysler Historical Foundation*

combustion chamber to exhaust the spent gasses. Low-friction, free-turning valve keepers allowed the valves to rotate freely, minimizing warping, sticking, and wear. Heads were cast of high-alloy material providing integral valve guides and seats. Hydraulic tappets provided adjustment-free operation, the camshaft (also made of high-test alloy cast iron) mounted in five bearings, driven by a heavy-duty silent chain drive. Carburetion came from a dual down-draft carburetor, each throat feeding four-cylinders through a double-deck intake manifold. Automatic choke, automatic manifold heat control, and a heavy-duty oil bath air cleaner were standard equipment, as was the fuel tank mounted Oilite fuel filter. The V-8–like the six long before it–relied on aluminum-alloy pistons, featuring a slipper skirt design. Unlike the six, only three rings were fitted to each piston. Borrowing a page from the racing fraternity, Plymouth V-8s featured two breaker points in the distributor delivering a hotter spark to special resistor spark plugs.

An anti-kickout device on the starter prevented "false starts," cutting off the flow of electricity to accessories while the combination ignition-key/starter was being held open. A 45amp generator, with thermostatic control from the regulator upping output to 57amps during cold weather starts, was deemed adequate for all 1955 models. A bypass system to circulate water inside the engine while the thermostat was closed was a feature borrowed from the six, but new to the system was a special Pressure-Vent radiator cap. Under normal operating conditions a vent remained open allowing the engine to operate at atmospheric pressure. As coolant approached the boiling point, the valve closed, putting the system under pressure (thus raising the boiling point) and preventing loss of engine

coolant. A radiator fan shroud allowed the fan to draw more air through the radiator (Plymouth was the only car in the low-priced field so equipped). A replaceable oil filter element and crankcase ventilation completed the V-8 package.

Continuing the transmission options of the year before, both the six and V-8 could be coupled to the two-speed PowerFlite automatic. Several improvements, including a different transmission input shaft and reaction shaft and seal, were made to the PowerFlite unit for 1955, requiring transmission rebuilders to follow the transmission date codes when replacing parts.

Leading Plymouth's accessory list this year was co-axial power steering, a $96.50 option. Requiring only four turns lock-to-lock, the Plymouth system was an integral part of the car, not an added-on unit like most of the competition, the power steering unit contained within the steering column (only the pump was mounted outside of the steering column). Like its corporate brethren, Plymouth's power steering was oft criticized for its lack of "road feel." Other accessories included power brakes (MoPar Parts released a dealer-installed power brake unit in November 1954 that could be retrofitted to all models back to 1951 as a $46.75 option.), a power two-way seat providing 5in of forward movement and 1-1/8in of lift (of the low-priced three, only Ford offered a four-way power seat), power windows on all models (Chevy offered them on its Bel Air and 210 models only, Ford only its Fairlane and Custom), and Airtemp air conditioning.

The Airtemp system mounted the condenser and compressor under the hood, the receiver under the floor of the car, and the evaporator beneath the package shelf in the trunk. Two outside air scoops, located just aft of the rear window, drew fresh air into the system. Vents mounted on the package shelf inside the car forced air up and over the seat to the front of the car, circulating fresh air through the car every 30sec.

Sales of the 1955 models took off like a rocket. From the doldrums of late 1954, production leapfrogged to 2,400 cars per day, running three shifts (although the third shift was manned by a skeleton crew) including Saturdays. Chrysler Corporation sales (all lines enjoyed the new Exner styling) jumped 40 percent over 1954, the corporation grabbing 18.5 percent of the new car market (compared to just 13 percent during 1954). Jack Mansfield, Plymouth's president, told *Motor Trend* magazine in February that he had never seen anything like it in thirty years in the automobile business. Production during December (1954) was 78,000 units, the biggest single month in Plymouth history. Mansfield set his eyes on 726,000 cars for 1955, a record if it were to happen and double of last year's sales. In the same issue of *Motor Trend*,

L.L. Colbert, Chrysler's president flat out claimed, "We're very serious about putting Plymouth back in third place." The corporation had a quarter million backlogged orders for cars! Buick remained in the fray, and by the end of January 1955 Buick remained ahead of Plymouth by a scant 1,800 retail deliveries. Both manufacturers were running at all-time highs.

By May dealers were being told to steer prospective customers toward 6-cylinder cars as Dodge was unable to keep up with demand for V-8s; likewise, buyers wanting PowerFlite were discouraged for the same reason.

Taking Walter Chrysler's 1932 sales slogan to heart, Detroit's largest Plymouth dealer, Petzold Motor Sales Company asked customers to "Look At All Three," boldly displaying, side by side on the showroom floor, a 1955 Plymouth, 1955 Ford, and 1955 Chevrolet sedan. Outside, a fleet of demonstrators comprised of all three makes awaited test drives by prospective customers. When asked the results of this method of selling, Tom Petzold claimed buyers chose Plymouth by a wide margin.

Road testers had a field day comparing the new models. *Motor Trend* named Plymouth (when equipped with power steering) the "Easiest Car To Drive" of all the 1955 models. *Motor Trend* pitted a $2,260 Belvedere V-8 equipped with PowerFlite against a $2,096 Chevrolet 210 V-8 sedan with Powerglide and a $2,123 Ford Customline V-8 with Fordomatic. In the 0–60mph contest Chevrolet racked up top honors at 12.3sec, compared to Plymouth's 13.2sec and Ford's 14.5sec runs. Quarter mile times for the trio saw Plymouth (with the longest elapsed time) take top speed honors with a run of 20.3sec at 98.4mph, compared to the Chevy's 19sec 97.3mph and Ford's 19.4sec 95.2 mph dash.

Gas mileage tests at a steady 60mph put Plymouth in the middle with a reading of 15.2mpg; Chevrolet took top honors with a 15.8mpg reading, Ford placing third at 14mpg. Later in the year *Motor Trend* tested a 167hp V-8 Belvedere sedan against a Belvedere convertible fitted with the 177hp engine. Despite the convertible's weight disadvantage (due to its heavier frame) it still outperformed the sedan. The convertible managed a 13.1sec 0–60mph time compared to the sedan's 13.2sec run. Quarter mile times showed similar results–the convertible hitting 74mph in 19.7sec, the sedan 69.5mph in 20.3sec. Mileage (figured on a trip basis rather than steady speed) showed the sedan averaging 15mpg over 1,134mi vs. the convertible's 14mpg reading for 609mi.

By the time the 1955 model year drew to a close, Plymouth had nearly met Jack Mansfield's 726,000 car prediction–ending the year with 705,455 cars (including 1,000 Canadian-built 6-cylinder Belvederes). The 1950 production record

Plymouth added a four-door station wagon to the list for 1955—the first four-door wagon since the woody wagon of 1950. *Chrysler Historical Foundation*

had been broken, but Buick still remained in third place. Nearly 48 percent of Plymouths built had been V-8 equipped. Thirty-nine percent of buyers had chosen the top line Belvedere series (61 percent with V-8s). Savoy sales amounted to 34 percent of production (41 percent with V-8s). The bottom-line Plaza accounted for 27 percent of total sales, with 70 percent of all Plazas sold equipped with the 6-cylinder engine. Station wagon sales had risen to nearly 10 percent of production.

Nineteen-fifty-five proved to be a high water mark for the entire industry, calendar year sales amounting to better than 7,920,000 cars. The only question that remained now was what could Plymouth do for 1956?

1956: The Ship Becomes A Plane

Chevrolet, Ford, and Plymouth all entered 1956 with mildly restyled facelifts of the new cars introduced the year before. The new Ford and Chevys relied mainly on revamped side trim, grilles, and taillamps to set them apart from 1955's cars. Like the others, Plymouth retained the old body, but added new quarter panels to dramatically change the overall shape of the body to what Exner called "airfoil" styling. One inch longer than the 1955 and slimmer and taller, the airfoil fenders trailed off into space "leaving no question that the car is racing forward," according to the data book. Slashed at a steep angle, the fenders gave the car a "flying away" look when viewed from the side or the rear. Airfin taillights, slim and tapered to emphasize the height

Marketplace (Calendar Year 1956)
Chevrolet–26.3 percent
Ford–23.1 percent
Plymouth–8.1 percent

Powell - The Recycled Plymouth

Hayward and Channing Powell were two of many who attempted to capitalize on the post-war seller's market. Everyone it seems, had their idea of what should have been the next "Model T." Few managed to get off the ground at all, let alone build any automobiles, but there were exceptions—and the pickup built by the Powell Brothers would be one of the most successful.

Unlike most of the post-war ventures, the Powell was a full-sized automobile. And the Powell was unique—rather than starting from scratch, it was based on recycled components, and was in reality, a brand-new "used" car.

The Powell Brothers got their start in the Los Angeles area around 1926. They dabbled in electronics, but were best-known for the motor scooters they built before and immediately after WWII.

Material shortages brought on by America's involvement in the Korean conflict, followed by a flood of imported scooters, found the Powells turning their attention elsewhere.

Around 1950 they laid out plans for a passenger-car-like pickup, which in 1952, they built on a six-cylinder Chevrolet chassis. The vehicle's styling was

Powell Sport Wagons carried these nameplates on each front fender.

Early Powells had wooden front and rear bumpers until some states declared them illegal. Owner: Jim Berka.

rather straightforward, featuring smooth, free-flowing lines from front to back, which may have been more the result of necessity than design as the Powells' body was hand built in their shop. The greenhouse of this first pickup, dubbed the "Sport Wagon," resembled an airplane cockpit of the era, and in fact, many aircraft construction techniques were applied in building the first prototype and subsequent production models.

Although briefly sidetracked by another project, the Powells ultimately decided to stake their fortune on their original idea of a passenger car-based pickup.

The first major consideration was on what chassis the pickup would be based. Although a Ford V-8-powered chassis was considered, the ultimate decision was made in favor of Plymouth's 1941 chassis powered by the L-head, six-cylinder engine. No doubt Plymouth's open drive shaft, superior hydraulic brakes, and independent suspension had much to do with the Powell's final choice. In addition, a six would be economical to operate. As a bonus, Chrysler offered great interchangability of parts between all its lines.

The 117in wheelbase 1941 Plymouth chassis would provide a sturdy platform for the addition of the Powell-built all-steel body. At 2,700lb, the Powell Sport Wagon pickup weighed about 200lb less than a standard Plymouth sedan.

Production of Powell Sport Wagons began in October 1954. A Gardena wrecking yard, Schulberg Auto Wreckers, supplied the Powells with more than 2,000 Plymouth chassis, at a cost of $45 each (later raised to $65). Once at the Powell factory, the Plymouth chassis was stripped to its essential components; chassis and suspension components were rebuilt, and the engine removed and sent to Engine Rebuilding Corporation in Los Angeles. (Powell literature claimed Plymouth engines were always used, but existing Powells prove that any usable MoPar engine might be used).

Riding on 6.00x16in Goodyear blackwall tires, a completed pickup stood 68in high, 71in wide, and 168in long. The building of a Sport Wagon was a rather interesting attempt at "real" production. The all-steel body was built in-house using special jigs to ensure proper panel alignment. Unlike other pickups

New for 1956 was the Powell Sport Wagon station wagon.

of the era, the box was integral with the cab. In a departure from the 1952 prototype, production pickup eliminated the small quarter windows behind the doors, probably as a cost-cutting move. Doors were fitted with sliding glass panels rather than roll-down windows, again presumably to cut costs.

Prototype and early production Sport Wagons were fitted with varnished oak bumpers and tailgate, but the bumpers were changed when it was discovered some states did not consider them legal. The lift-out tailgate was also changed to steel, and door check straps were added early in production; previously, front doors could arc 180 degrees until flush with the front fenders.

The front nose panel was constructed of fiberglass molded by a boat repair shop in nearby Paramount, California, and was decorated by three horizontal chrome strips (pirated from the rear door of 1950 Ford sedans) and a Powell nameplate. These nameplates also appeared on the lower portion of the front fenders, behind the wheel openings. Body sides on Deluxe pickups were adorned with a single full-length chrome strip, again pirated from a 1950 Ford two door. The hood opened in the old-fashioned butterfly style. One of the earliest known existing Powells differs from later versions by having a riveted, rather than spot-welded body. It would appear that few of these riveted bodies, which also had cowl ventilators, were built, and the change to spot welding, along with other improvements were noted by a new serial number sequencing, starting at PMC-2000. The Powell-assigned serial number can be found on the frame, where the front cross-member forms a Y with the right frame channel.

Interiors were spartan, with 57in wide seats made from new foam rubber covered with heavy vinyl upholstery. The stock 1941 Plymouth instrument cluster was fitted into the Powell-designed, silver-gray hammertone finish dash. Each Sport Wagon received a new wiring harness, fabricated in the Powell factory. Door panels on early models were hammertone-painted Masonite panels though later station wagons had real upholstery. There was no glove compartment as such, just an open tray stretching the width of the instrument panel. Reflecting its California heritage, no provision was made for a heater or defroster, and a single electric windshield wiper was standard (dual wipers came standard on the wagon).

In 1955, the only options offered, other than two-tone paint, were turn signals and chrome wheel discs. A "Deluxe" version appeared for 1956 that included turn signals, a diamond plate rear bumper and tailgate, and two-tone vinyl upholstery. Perhaps the most novel feature of the Sport Wagon was the optional "fishing pole" holder that could be built into the rear fender panels. Seven inches in diameter and 6-1/2ft long, the lockable troughs were perfect for carrying long items such as fishing poles, rifles, and tubing. Access to items was as easy as pulling the tray out from the rear.

Another option designed with the sportsman in mind was the Powell-built pop-up camper topper. Constructed of wood, the $295 camper added 300lb to the pickup and could be easily installed or removed by two men. Hinged at the front, the camper provided nearly 6ft of headroom in the "up" position and came equipped with two fold-down cots.

Advertised as the only new car in America for less than $1,000 in 1955, a Sport Wagon listed for $998.87. Prices rose slightly for 1956, to $1,095 for the Standard model and $1,198 for the Deluxe. The Sport Wagons were sold through franchised dealers and each came with the then standard 90-day/4000mi guarantee. Service was available through any Chrysler agency. Because of the Powells' California assembly and distribution, few were sold east of the Rockies.

The pickup was joined by a station wagon in 1956. Priced at $1,675, wagon production never matched that of the pickup. Standard wagon equipment included a luggage rack on the roof, two "utility bins" and an interior of two-tone nylon or vinyl plastic covering. Lowering the rear seat provided a 48x80in

The station wagon's tailgate hinged at the roof. Wagons had two utility trays, one on either side of the body. Pickup buyers got one tray on the right side, with the left side optional.

After selling the Alameda Avenue building, the Powells moved to this building on Firestone Boulevard. All that remains today is this painted sign on the rear of the building. *Bill Hossfield*

cargo area. The rear bumper was specially made to accommodate a trailer hitch ball. Standard colors on all body styles were red, yellow, white, or sea green or two-tone combinations. The wagon had a one-piece tailgate, hinged at the roof. Both body styles carried the spare tire in its own compartment beneath the floor of the bed, with an access door directly above the rear bumper.

Motor Life, in its October 1955 issue, reported over 300 Sport Wagons had been sold, with production at the Compton facility running about three completed vehicles per day with a potential of up to ten per day. Although no production figures were ever released it would appear about 1,000 pickups and 300 station wagons comprised total production.

Motor Trend's Walt Woron road tested a Sport Wagon pickup with pop-up camper for that magazine's February 1956 issue. Woron took the Powell on a 700mi trip into the mountains in near-zero temperatures. The Powell averaged 15.1mpg but Woron felt that under "normal" conditions it probably would deliver 17mpg. *Motor Life* quoted a 20mpg figure in their earlier test. The only negative point in Woron's report was high oil consumption—two quarts in 700mi—despite the fact the engine was supposed to have had a 2,500mi break-in prior to his taking delivery. Woron wrote, "The lasting impression I have from the Powell Sport Wagon is that I was driving a passenger car with most of the advantages of a pickup truck—without any of the disadvantages."

The Powell factory in full swing early in 1956. *Bob D'Olivia*

94

By early 1957, Powell Manufacturing Company was coming unglued. Hayward and Channing found themselves at odds with the government over non-payment of an 8 percent excise tax they had either ignored or had not realized they were required to pay. The Powell brothers found their venture in the hands of the courts. With assets frozen, the March 1, 1957, balance sheet showed assets of $102,387.94 against liabilities of $98,803.90.

At a meeting of the Creditors Committee, Hayward and Channing were given until April I to present a reorganization or refinancing proposal. When

MANUFACTURING COMPANY

2914 NORTH ALAMEDA STREET • **COMPTON CALIFORNIA** • **TELEPHONE NEVADA 6-1729**

INFORMATION and SPECIFICATIONS

on the

P O W E L L   "Custom Built"   S P O R T   W A G O N

Appearance: The Powell Sport Wagon has an outstanding appearance and is one of the most beautiful on the market. It comes in a variety of beautiful 1955 colors with sparkling chrome trim. The smooth flowing lines are not so extreme in style that they will become out of date. The Powell Sport Wagon has been designed to last both in performance and appearance.

Uses: Ideally suited for sports of all kinds, week-end camping trips, longer trips, shopping, general utility, a family runabout and a perfect second car. Rides like a sedan and drives like a sports car.

Body: All steel welded body.   Bumpers and tail gate are varnished oak.

Bed Size: 4 x 6 feet.   Seat Width: 58 inches; seat cushions and back of seat are deep air foam rubber.

Overall Height: 5 feet 8 inches.   Overall Length: 14 feet 9 inches.

Wheel Base: 117 inches,   Tires: 600 x 16 4-Ply Goodyear Tires.

Unladen Weight: 2700 pounds.   Capacity: Rated as 1/4 Ton Pick-up; Overload springs available for extra loads.

Engine: The Powell "Custom Built" Sport Wagon is built on a Plymouth chassis. The Powell's low price is made possible by unique engineering features reflecting sensational economies achieved through the miracle of modern remanufacturing techniques. The rugged 6-cylinder in-line 90-horsepower engine is in a standard Plymouth power plant remanufactured to exacting tolerances that are equivalent to, and in some instances even exceeding, new engine specifications.

Price: The Powell Sport Wagon sells for $998.87 at the factory plus Sales Tax (in California) and license. Sold with standard motor car guarantee.

Price sheet for the 1955 Powell models. *Jeff Peterson*

and sweep of the rear fenders, and a "jet-like tube" back-up lamp housing all emphasized the aeronautical theme of the car. New body moldings, especially those of the Belvedere, emphasized the "aerodynamic, ready for take off" look. Topping off each

rear fender was Exner's new "Forward Look" emblem on Belvedere and Sport Suburban models.

Front sheet metal changed little from previous models, but the design tended to complement the extended rear quarters. The fenders thrust forward, canting back as they fell closer to the bumper. A slightly revised grille bar featured a grid pattern in the center of the bar, adorned with a gold V when the car was equipped with V-8 power. Trusting that everyone knew what make of car it was, the word Plymouth appeared only on the hood.

The new design also called for a break with tradition—for the first time since 1928, the Mayflower sailing ship did not appear on the front of the car, being replaced by a "jet plane hood ornament—pointing up the fast, forward flow of body lines." For the traditionalist, the jet plane was the same abstract boat that had been used in 1955, with the addition of a pair of wings to turn it magically into a jet plane. Appearing on the bottom of the hood and on the deck lid ornaments were Plymouth's coat of arms. The deck lid ornament continued to use two styles—a V for cars with V-8 engines and a straight bar for 6-cylinder cars. There were also new pull-type exterior door handles, replacing 1955's one-year-only push-button handles. Unseen, but a sell-

The Mayflower sailing ship had now become a "jet plane." The Plymouth crest moved down to the "tooth" in the center of the hood. V-8-powered cars had a "V" mounted on the grille mesh, while 6-cylinder cars, such as this, were plain. *William A.C. Pettit III*

ing point, were new safeguard door latches that placed a U-shaped striker of heavy-gauge metal on the door pillar into an interlocking "U" on the door latch. These interlocking "U"s prevented fore and aft separation of the latch from the door post in crash situations.

Plaza and Savoy models had to settle for side trim virtually unchanged from 1955. The rather busy and unusual Belvedere side trim incorporated a straight spear running from the leading edge of the front fender to the rear edge of the front door. Several inches below this another straight spear ran from the center of the front door back to the back-up light housing. The two were connected by a dog-leg horizontal piece and a heavy medallion bearing the word "Belvedere." Once again this layout provided the basis for Sportone two-tone paint combinations. By October MoPar released a Sportone molding package for in-field installation on all Plaza and Savoy models. These moldings differed only in not having the model name on the side medallion, retailing for $16 and $27 per package depending on body style.

Plymouth engineers had been equally busy with the car's interior. Answering complaints about the placement of the oil pressure and temperature gauges in front of the passenger, Plymouth moved them in front of the driver. On the downside, they were changed from readable gauges to "idiot"

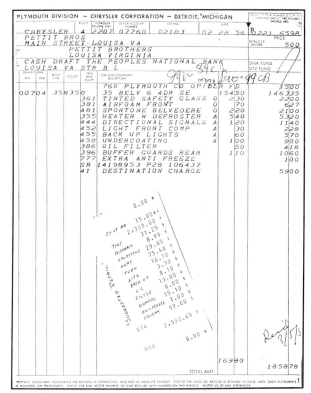

A Plymouth invoice to a Virginia dealer shows his cost on a 6-cylinder Belvedere four-door sedan. The till tape overlay indicates the car's retail price. *William A.C. Pettit III*

Answering customers' complaints about the location of the temperature and oil gauges on 1955 models, Plymouth turned them into red "idiot" lights in front of the driver, placing the heater controls on the passenger side instead. *William A.C. Pettit III*

lights. Because the dash panel had gone unchanged, there was no room for the gauges in front of the driver, hence the switch to warning lights. Replacing the gauges in front of the passenger were the heater-defroster controls—a move that made them unhandy for the driver. These controls had been mounted on the lower left corner of the dash, where the transmission controls now lived.

The 1955 Plymouth had shocked the motoring world by sticking the automatic transmission control lever through the dashboard near the driver's right knee cap. For 1956, Plymouth drivers had to learn to use their left hand for this operation as Plymouth (and the rest of the corporation's cars) went to push-button shifting on automatic cars. Push-button transmissions were the rage during the late 1950s—Mercury, Edsel, Rambler, and Packard all had their fling with push-button controls. Of the lot, only Chrysler's was mechanically controlled and virtually trouble free. Regardless, Chrysler's

"typewriter" transmission controls were a love it or hate it proposition. The push-button transmission would remain a Chrysler hallmark until 1965, when it was abandoned in favor of (and under government edict to standardize shift quadrants throughout the industry) the normal shift lever on the steering column.

Plymouth entered 1956 with virtually the same model line-up as 1955. 6-cylinder cars were coded as the P28 series, V-8 cars as P29s. Again, the suffix number indicated the car's model. Plazas were either P28-1 or P29-1, Savoys P28-2 or P29-2, and Belvederes P28-3 or P29-3.

At the top of the line was the Belvedere series, available in four-door, club sedan (two-door), sport coupe, or convertible coupe body styles. New for the year was Plymouth's first Sport Sedan, a true four-door hardtop. Plymouth stressed this new model was full size, giving front and rear seat passengers the same room as a sedan in an open

Automatic transmission cars had the controls mounted to the driver's left and used push buttons to select gears. The "type-writer" controls would be used through 1964. *Chrysler Historical Foundation*

model. To achieve the open air status, the rear window was a complicated two-piece affair. When the window was being opened, the rear section arced forward and down, while the front section moved rearward slightly and then straight down. The Sport Sedan sold reasonably well but still managed to outsell only the convertible in the Belvedere line-up. The Sport Sedan, like the rest of the Belvedere line, was offered with either 6- or 8-cylinder power, with the exception of the Belvedere convertible which mandated eight cylinders.

Savoy buyers had the choice of a four-door sedan, club sedan (two door), and a sport coupe in either 6- or 8-cylinder form. Plaza buyers were also given the choice of 6- or 8-cylinder power in the three models offered, which included a four door, club sedan (two door), or business coupe. Like the club sedan, the business coupe was a two door designed for the traveling salesman. It came without a rear seat, but could be ordered with a V-8.

Station wagon buyers were given four choices as wagon sales continued to grow (to better than 14 percent of total 1956 production). Corresponding to the Belvedere line was the Sport Suburban four-door wagon. Next in line was the Custom Suburban, again a four door. The Custom Suburban line also included a two-door wagon, as was the bottom-of-the-line Deluxe Suburban wagon. All four wagons could be had with either 6- or 8-cylinder power.

Upholstery materials continued to receive much attention; Belvederes received seats upholstered in key-pattern Aztec cloth, with seatback inserts of pleated satin vinyl. The pleated vinyl was placed as an insert in the all-vinyl side trim with floors covered in carpet. Belvedere convertible buyers had the choice of Aztec cloth and satin vinyl or all-vinyl upholstery. Convertible tops could be had in white, black, blue, or green. The Belvedere interiors came in four "fashion-matched" colors, including two-tone green, two-tone blue, brown with cream, or black and rose. A fifth combination included black cloth with white vinyl and a gray headliner. Belvedere Sport Sedans boasted an exclusive upholstery pattern of Mosaic Weave with Satin vinyl bolsters, a combination repeated on the door panels with harmonizing floor carpeting. Sport Sedan combinations included two-tone green, two-tone turquoise, black with rose, brown with cream, and black and white.

Savoy upholstery included Sorrento Stripe cloth in combination with Satin vinyl bolsters. Door and side panels featured a central insert of pleated vinyl with satin vinyl above and below, while floors were covered in a color-matched rubber mat. The Savoy line offered four color combinations of two-tone green, two-tone blue, brown with cream, and gray with charcoal. Plaza buyers were offered just three color combinations—two-tone

Upholstery detail of the 1956 Belvedere sedan. *William A.C. Pettit III*

green, two-tone blue, and light gray with silver "Plazacord" accented by satin vinyl bolsters on seat cushions and seatbacks. Door and side panels were finished in matching Satin vinyl with floors covered with black rubber mats. Plaza and Savoy club sedan and four-door sedan buyers (along with Plaza business coupe buyers) could opt for a tan all-vinyl leatherette at additional cost.

Sport Suburbans found seats upholstered in Sportspun Tweed enriched with metallic threads on the seatback inserts and central side panels. Seatbacks, seat cushion facings, and lower door panels

"Forward Look" emblems appeared on the fin on all Belvedere models. Owner: Bill Brown. *Jim Benjaminson*

This top-of-the-line Belvedere sedan sports standard equipment "dog dish" hubcaps. Owner: William A. C. Pettit III.

were of Stardust Vinyl, with headliners of Royalite. Cargo areas were covered with ribbed Vinoleum (a vinyl coated linoleum). Front floors were covered with a tan rubber mat. This brown-beige seat and door panel combination was featured in all Sport

This Savoy Club Sedan with Sportone trim has its lower body painted to match the roof color. Owner: Thomas Cieszkowski.

Suburban models with garnish moldings and instrument panel painted in green, turquoise, brown, or black to match the exterior color of the car. Custom Suburbans, in either two- or four-door body styles, had completely different patterns in Ventilating Vinyl, a woven cloth faced with vinyl in a "golf-tee" pattern. Door panels were also all vinyl with Satin vinyl in the upper section and pleated vinyl below. Floors were covered with either black or tan mats while the cargo area was covered with beige Vinoleum. Upholstery colors included brown with cream, two-tone green, and black with silver. Headliners were again of Royalite in either beige, green, or gray.

Reflecting its bottom-of-the-line status, two-door Deluxe Suburban buyers were given a single charcoal-gray textured vinyl upholstery with bolsters of silver-gray satin vinyl in a distinctive V pattern. Door and side panels were also textured vinyl while the headliner was gray Royalite. Unlike the other wagons in the line-up both the floor and cargo areas of the Deluxe Suburban were covered with black rubber mats.

Chassis-wise the 1956 Plymouth was little more than a clone of the 1955s. Six-cylinder cars were fitted with 10in brakes front and rear, V-8 cars got 11in brakes on the front only, and station wagons wore 11in brakes all the way around. Gear ratios were 3.73 on standard transmission and PowerFlite 6-cylinder cars, 3.54 on PowerFlite V-8s, and 4.1

with overdrive. Plymouth continued to mount its parking brake on the transmission, relying on the tried and true external contracting brake band on standard shift cars. PowerFlite, due to its method of construction, had an internal expanding parking brake. Power brakes continued to be a popular option, with Plymouth offering two versions, including a new air-suspended system for PowerFlite cars (with an 8in wide brake pedal sitting 4-1/2in above the floor) and the old vacuum-suspended type for standard transmission cars (with a pedal 6in off the floor to match the clutch pedal height). The Power-Flite brake system included a reserve tank mounted on the left fenderwell under the hood.

The big news under the hood was Plymouth's new Hy-Fire V-8–this time its own engine designed and built by Plymouth. In many respects the new engine was much like the old one and even looked the same (the new engine was most identifiable by its saw-toothed valve covers). Plymouth engineers made the block slightly longer, with more "meat"

between the cylinder bores, installed a larger crank-shaft with larger bearings, and enlarged the valve ports for better breathing.

The new 277ci 187hp engine was exclusive to Belvedere and Sport Suburbans and had a bore and stroke of 3.75x3.13in; the old "Dodge" 270ci 180hp Hy-Fire was carried over for use in Plaza and Savoy models. Both engines shared an 8:1 compression ratio and developed their maximum horsepower at 4400rpm. For those wanting more power, the 277 was available with a power pack that included a four-barrel carburetor and dual exhausts and developed an even 200hp. Later in the model year, a potent 303ci engine would make its appearance in the Fury. This engine, which had grown to 318ci by 1957, would continue in use through 1967 before seeing any major revisions. By year's end, fully 60 percent of Plymouth's 1956 production would be fitted with V-8s. The new V-8 made its first public appearance three weeks prior to the unveiling of the new models at the NHRA Nationals

As one of the first major corporations to recognize the fledgling National Hot Rod Association, Plymouth gave NHRA this 1955 Plaza V-8 station wagon which was used by the organization's safety officer (Bud Coons, left). On its 1955 "Drag Safari" the wagon pulled an equipment-filled trailer to drag meets around the country. Plymouth expanded its support in 1956, donating a pair of station wagons and a Fury hardtop for NHRA personnel use. Participants at the 1956 Great Bend, Kansas, national drag meet also vied for Plymouth V-8 engines given as prizes.

held in Great Bend, Kansas. Plymouth offered a special prize of a brand new 277ci V-8 to the hot-rodder posting the fastest time with a Plymouth.

Despite the industry-wide popularity of V-8s, 40 percent of Plymouth buyers chose the tried and true 230ci "PowerFlow" six Plymouth shared with Dodge. The Dodge version, with a two-barrel carburetor, pumped out 131hp at 3600rpm. Plymouth's single-barrel version could muster only 125hp. Not to be outdone, Plymouth offered buyers a Power Pack for the six. Consisting of a Stromberg dual throat carburetor, special intake manifold, larger air cleaner and a 3.9 rear-axle ratio, Power-Flow with Power Pack raised Plymouth's horsepower to 131. Highly sought after by today's enthusiasts, the 6-cylinder power pack is very rare.

As the demand made by more electrical accessories grew, it became apparent the old 6-volt system could no longer suffice–for 1956 it was abandoned in favor of 12-volt electrics. An increased capacity generator and new starting motor were part of the system. Long-reach resistor spark plugs, a single-point distributor, and weatherproofed ignition helped ensure reliable performance of the system during wet weather conditions.

Plymouth also continued to offer special packages for police and taxi use (1956 marked the first use of specially prepared sales catalogs for the taxi market). As usual, these packages included heavy-duty chassis springs, heavy-duty shock absorbers, heavier gauge wire springs in the seat and seatback cushions, battery heat shields, and a 70amp-hour battery. Straight stick cars with PowerFlow used a 10in clutch plate, while V-8 cars used an 11in clutch. All 6-cylinder taxis fitted with the heavy-duty clutch also received a special cylinder head raising compression to 7.9:1 (this head, part number 1676377, replaced the regular head part number 1616823). Individual items available at extra cost on these packages included a rear-seat ashtray on Plaza and Deluxe Suburbans, 11in front brakes on 6-cylinder taxicabs, two special "city traffic" Carter carburetors on 6-cylinder cars (Carter models 2063 S or 2063 SA and Carter 2062 S and 2062 SA), a 20gal capacity gas tank (recommended for use only on taxis), a Handy governor on 6-cylinder cars, automatic dome light switches on rear doors, and a variety of heavy-duty generators for police work.

Power steering, power brakes, and air conditioning were becoming more common, but highlighting the accessory group was "Hiway Hi-Fi," a record player for a car. Hiway Hi-Fi originally required ordering the new Electro Touch-Tune

Helping to free Plymouth from its "Old Maid" reputation was the fire-breathing Fury, available only as a white two-door hardtop with gold anodized side and grille trim, gold hood ornament, and gold trimmed "turbine blade" hubcaps. Owner: Loyd Groshong. *Jim Benjaminson*

Model 916 radio. Later, the system would work with any 800 or 900 series radio offered in any Chrysler product. Utilizing special records and a needle that wasn't supposed to skip on rough roads, the records turned at just 16-2/3rpm. At $56.95 (which included six records), plus $2.55 for the mounting bracket, Hiway Hi-Fi wasn't terribly expensive, but the market for a car record player never really existed, making Hiway Hi-Fi units extremely rare today. The same unit was available across the board for all Chrysler cars and lasted through the 1960 model year before being discontinued.

Things were changing at Plymouth. The image of the old maid's car was being turned around. And helping change that image was Plymouth's 1956 introduction of the hairy-chested Fury. Tom MaCahill probably said it best when he wrote in the September 1956 issue of *Mechanix Illustrated*, "Five years ago, if performance figures such as these were pub-

lished for a full-sized Plymouth, I'd have been whipped into a straitjacket and mailed to the nearest headshrinkers convention." What MaCahill was crowing about was Plymouth's entry into the muscle car field—an egg-shell white two-door hard top garnished with gold anodized aluminum and called, simply, Fury.

The hood nameplate and ornament, grille insert, and turbine wheel covers were gold. Even the interior wore the gold and white theme; the seat insets featuring a golden metallic thread against white bolsters, with window garnish moldings in shiny chrome plate. The instrument panel was based on the Belvedere sport coupe and remained unchanged with one exception: a small 6000rpm tachometer located inconveniently by the ignition switch.

Under the hood was a Canadian-sourced 303ci V-8 pumping out an honest 240hp at 4800rpm. A bore and stroke of 3-13/16x3-5/16in produced

The four-door Sport Suburban station wagon was trimmed like the Belvedere. *Chrysler Historical Foundation*

As evidenced by this prototype, Plymouth toyed with the idea of re-entering the sedan delivery market in 1955. Both Chevrolet and Ford offered similar body styles but sales were never strong for either one. *Chrysler Historical Foundation*

compression of 9.25:1, and air and fuel were mixed by a single Carter WCFB 2442 S four-barrel carburetor. Reinforced dome pistons, a high-performance camshaft, high-load valve springs, balanced connecting rods, and high-speed distributor rounded out the engine package. Horsepower reached the

The Sedan delivery idea was still being considered as the 1956s came to market, but the car never went into production. *Chrysler Historical Foundation*

road through either a standard transmission backed by a heavy-duty 10in Borg & Beck clutch and pressure plate or a heavy-duty PowerFlite automatic designed for use in big Dodges. Furys rode on 7.10x15in 4-ply nylon cord black sidewall tires mounted on 5-1/2in rims. The standard rear-end ratio was 3.73 with options of 3.54, 3.9, 4.1, or 4.3:1. Heavy-duty (six leaves) springs were fitted front and rear. Eleven-inch brakes at all four corners brought the car to a halt, and heavy-duty sway bars helped the big Plymouth track a straight line down the road. The Fury sat 1in lower than its Belvedere stable mate, giving the car a leaner appearance.

"The Fury is a small 300B," MaCahill wrote, referring to Chrysler's muscle car. Unlike the Chrysler 300s, which cleaned up at the nation's race tracks during 1955 and 1956, the Fury achieved little racing success. The Fury had set a one-way record of 143.598mph on January 7 during the annual Daytona Beach Speed Week with a two-way average of 136.415mph. (Contradictory speeds were reported, ranging from 123.440 to 124.611 for the two-way average speed. While some cars that had participated were later declared illegal, the Fury's record was upheld when the car was certified legally stock.) Regardless, Plymouth had shattered the record previously held by Cadillac at 112.295mph.

For speed enthusiasts, Plymouth released a dealer-installed High Performance Package in the spring of 1956. Retailing for $746.90, the kit included dual four-barrels, special air cleaners, an aluminum intake manifold, high-performance camshaft and tappets, a hand choke assembly, and all necessary linkage to hook everything up. This kit was available for both the 277ci Belvedere V-8 and the Fury 303ci V-8. The kit raised the 277's horsepower to 230 while upping the Fury's to 270hp.

Motor Trend put the new Plymouth**s** to the test, pitting a 277ci Belvedere against a Fury and a Belvedere club sedan equipped with a McCulloch supercharger. The regular Belvedere ran 0–60mph in 11.9sec, the Fury in 9.5sec, and the supercharged car in 8.2sec. In the 1/4mi, the normally aspirated Belvedere reached 76mph in 18.9sec, and the Fury hit 83.5mph in 16.9sec. Both were again outclassed by the supercharged Belveredere which ran 84.8mph run at 16.7sec.

Further *Motor Trend* tests found the Belvedere would deliver 16.6mpg at a steady 60mph, recording the same as a Chevrolet Bel Air; both bested the Ford Fairlane's 16.1mpg. The only cars bettering these mileage figures were the Studebaker Champion with overdrive (21.7mpg), Rambler Custom (19.9mpg), Oldsmobile Super 88 (17.6mpg), and the Studebaker Golden Hawk (16.7mpg).

In top speed testing, Chevrolet took top honors at 108mph, followed closely by the 107.1mph Belvedere. Ford was way behind at 100.2mph.

Early in March, PowerFlite transmissions changed from malleable iron to aluminum carriers with transmissions date coded C-7-56 and later. This change required that aluminum carriers be fitted with proper replacement parts, which did not interchange with the iron carriers. About the same time PowerFlite and overdrive deck lid nameplates were discontinued on all models.

Shortly before the end of the model run "as a signal honor to St. Louis Plymouth dealers and salesmen whose records stand high among the nation's sales," Plymouth put out a regular Plymouth sedan with a new color scheme designed especially for the St. Louis market. The St. Louis Blues Special was painted white on the upper body with a Gazelle blue on the lower body and roof of the car. Featuring Sportone trim, the car was like any other Plymouth with the exception of the paint scheme, which could not be ordered anywhere else in the U.S. Manufactured at the Evansville plant, the St. Louis Blues Special retailed for $1,776, including heater, whitewall tires, two-tone paint, and Sportone trim. No records were kept as to how many St. Louis Blues Specials were built or sold.

In another paint-related episode, Detroit's Petzold Motors gained national attention by announc-

Plymouths were often converted to either Dodge or DeSoto products by the factory. Contrary to what some believe, the Plymouth assembly line did not shut down to switch over to "conversion" production. Shown here is a 1956 Dodge conversion being followed by a "normal" 1956 Plymouth. *Chrysler Historical Foundation*

Airfoil rear fenders were accented by the thin, vertical taillamps. The gas filler door rode on the right side. Note the 6-cylinder emblem on the deck lid. *William A.C. Pettit III*

ing that they would paint 100 Plymouths in glow-in-the-dark colors at no extra cost for an introductory period of two weeks. Developed by 3M, the glow-in-the-dark paint was sprayed over the regular finish. Available in green, blue, brown, and Magenta Red, the colors were claimed to be visible 1500–1700ft away at night compared to less than half that distance for normally painted vehicles. How many people took up Petzold on the offer was not noted and 3M's luminous paint never caught on, at least in the automobile industry.

The end of the model year was marked by an industry-wide downturn from the record year of 1955. Plymouth sales were off 37 percent, dropping from 1955's 743,000 cars to 571,000. As in 1955, Plymouth found itself in fourth place, trailing Chevrolet, Ford, and Buick. Nonetheless, one new Plymouth still rolled off the assembly line every 20sec (total assembly time per car was just 53min). Airfoil styling had come to Plymouth, pointing the way into the future—just how far into the future was just around the corner.

Diesel Plymouths

The mid-1950s are best remembered by enthusiasts as the beginnings of the horsepower race, tailfins, and chrome applied with a trowel. In the Chrysler Corporation laboratories, it was also a time of serious research into alternative forms of powering an automobile. This was not a search for economy, as gasoline was cheap and the Arab oil embargoes were decades away, but a search for viable alternatives to the piston-engine. Chrysler's gas turbine program drew reams of publicity, but in the long run, after spending millions of dollars over nearly three decades, the gas turbine program is no closer to production today than it was in the 1950s.

Taking a back seat to the turbine cars was Chrysler Corporation's work with diesel power. The diesel, despite the fact that it probably held greater production line potential than did the turbine, gathered barely more than passing mention in the trade press.

The April 1956 *Motor Trend* mentioned only "that Chrysler is offering a Perkins four-cylinder diesel engine in the Plymouth Belvedere as an alter-

The only clue to this car's power source is the word "diesel" written across the windshield. A team consisting of Perkins of England, Hunter N.V., and the Plymouth assembly plant in Antwerp, Belgium, converted a small number of cars such as this 1955 Belvedere sedan to diesel power. *Chrysler Historical Foundation*

native to the conventional gasoline engine." Three short lines most readers probably glanced over and quickly forgot.

Plymouth's diesel engine program was the collaboration of three companies: Perkins Diesel of Peterborough, England; Hunter N.V. of Antwerp, Belgium; and Chrysler's Antwerp subsidiary Societe Anonyme Chrysler. The Antwerp plant was among the oldest of Chrysler's overseas assembly plants, its main purpose to supply locally assembled Chrysler products to the European lowland countries.

Actual development of the Perkins diesel conversions was done by Hunter N.V. B. Geerstem, managing director of Hunter stated, "We developed the Plymouth conversion, based on P4 Perkins engines. A reasonable number were transformed in our own workshop. Most of them went to Belgian taxi companies and for many other professional uses."

Perkins P4 engines (Perkins had three "P" series engines in 3-, 4-, or 6-cylinder form) shared a common 5in stroke with a choice of 3-1/2in or 3-9/16in bore. Horsepower ratings, torque, and other data is unavailable. When Hunter began retrofitting Perkins into Plymouth sedans is uncertain—there is some indication the practice may have gone back as early as the P15 models of the late 1940s.

Proof of a Plymouth diesel's existence surfaced in the Chrysler Historical Foundation archives in 1988 when photos of a 1955 Belvedere sedan were found predating *Motor Trend*'s 1956 article. Except the word "DIESEL" written across the windshield, the car looked entirely stock. Interior photos of the same car revealed four control knobs—reading heat, start, idle, and stop—not found on regular Plymouths. Detailed photographs of the engine revealed a four-cylinder diesel. Outside of an additional 6-volt battery, the engine compartment was basically stock Plymouth.

While this particular 1955 may have been a one-off to test the feasibility of fitting the Perkins diesel, sources indicate that about 100 1956 diesel-powered cars were built. In its February 1957 issue, *Motor Life* wrote, "Some experimental work has gone on in the past year with diesel-powered Plymouths in

Power came from a Perkins P4 four-cylinder diesel engine. *Chrysler Historical Foundation*

Modifications to the dash included special knobs to control engine functions including heat, idle, start, and stop. Note the speedometer marked in kilometers per hour. *Chrysler Historical Foundation*

Belgium. The research, involving about 100 limited-production units, was conducted by an English firm called Perkins, which has offices in Canada."

According to *Motor Life*, these 1956 diesel Plymouths sold for "about $750 over the cost of the same car equipped with a six-cylinder engine"—about $2,700 U.S. "The idea behind the whole project is to develop something in which the higher initial cost would be offset by lower operating expenses," the article said. This was a particularly viable concern in Europe where the price of gas was already high and oversized American-built cars were falling out of favor.

Perkins, which had branches in Canada, apparently saw to it that a handful of diesel-powered cars were shipped there, where at least one car has survived. The diesel experiment was considered enough of a success that plans were made to continue the project into 1957. The 1957 Plymouth, with its much lower hood line (which dictated a 'shallow" carburetor in regular production) was considered a

major challenge. "Whether or not the new combination will be placed upon the market—which might or might not extend to other countries—depends on test results," *Motor Life* commented. The October 1959 *Motor Life* later reported, "Plymouth diesels are being seen more and more in taxicab fleets from coast to coast. Under-hood unit is the Perkins diesel. While they may be successful in cab operations, where continuous running is a factor, they are unlikely to be worthwhile as a private vehicle. The added cost of diesel installation could not be offset by fuel savings in life of the engine."

Nothing more was reported on the project, and whatever development took place went unnoticed by the U.S. trade press. Hunter N.V. continued to make Perkins diesel conversions and still does to this day—a current project finding a Perkins 6.247-liter diesel placed into a Jaguar XJ6! During its heyday, even Valiants were commonly converted to diesel power.

The only known surviving Perkins diesel-powered Plymouth is this 1956 Savoy which surfaced in Canada. The grille is the same as that used on the DeSoto Diplomat (a Plymouth converted and sold as a DeSoto). Owner: Burnice Bamping.

The only external clue to the car's powerplant is this Perkins emblem on the deck lid. The regular deck lid ornament indicates that the car was built with a six. Owner: Burnice Bamping.

Chapter 5

1957–1959:
Recapturing Lost Ground

1957: Three Years Ahead

The ads trumpeted: "Suddenly - Its 1960!" and "1960-New, Plymouth is three full years ahead." "In one flaming moment," read another, "Plymouth leaps three full years ahead–the only car that dares to break the time barrier! The car you might have expected in 1960 is at your dealers today!" If the hyperbole was to be believed, the new Plymouths sitting in showrooms were originally intended as 1960 models. In an unprecedented move, Chrysler Corporation had completely revised all five of its car lines, scuttling after just two years the all-new bodies introduced in 1955. What the corporation trotted out in its place were Virgil Exner's best designs ever, not just catching up with perennial

---

Marketplace (Calendar Year 1957)
Ford–25 percent
Chevrolet–24.3 percent
Plymouth–10 percent

Under-bumper gravel pan was the only flaw in the design of the 1957 Plymouths. This is the later version pan. Owner: Brian MacKay.

styling giant General Motors, but leaving "the General" far behind.

The effect of the new Plymouth sent shock waves through the styling halls of both GM and Ford. One story told of GM styling boss Harley Earl walking into the office of Chevrolet exterior designer C.J. MacKichan, throwing a 1957 Plymouth catalog on his desk and asking bitterly, "Why don't you quit?" Dave Holls, now retired from GM design, recalled in a June 1992 *Collectible Automobile* interview the effect the 1957 Chrysler lineup had on GM, "I never thought we beat the Plymouth. I don't think anybody appreciated these cars as much as we did at GM." The effect of Exner's "Flite Sweep" styling caused GM to drop, after just one model year, its 1958 bodies and redesign an entirely new line of cars for 1959.

"The Forward Look of Motion," trumpeted the dealer data book in describing the new look. And nowhere was the forward look more evident than in the wedge-shaped silhouette of the car. Low front fenders and hood, gently sloped windshield, a razor thin flat roof with tapered rear window, and rising fins created the wedge effect. Convertibles and hardtops complemented the styling best, four-door sedans probably compromising it at its worst. Station wagons, which usually adapted worst to a design, came off sleeker looking than the sedans.

If the 1956 Plymouth had been airplane inspired, the 1957 clearly took its cues from space ships–from the eye-browed headlights to the unobstructed greenhouse to the smooth clean sculptured sides, the idea of an earthbound space vehicle was everywhere. A redesigned, flatter, wider, lower frame and a switch to 14in wheels helped drop the 1957 Plymouth 5in lower than comparable 1956 models. A longer wheelbase, up 3in to 118in (122in for station wagons), was still 1/2in shorter than the 1949–52 cars, although few would have believed it when comparing the two cars side by side. Likewise the 1957 was actually shorter than the 1956 it replaced! Later in the year (during May production) the frame was changed, the inner side of the box section on both rails discontinued at a point beginning at the rear spring hanger and extending forward about 18in to the frame kick-up section.

Everything had been done to make the car look long, low, and wide. The hood effectively split the "almost" dual headlights at their center line. Original plans had called for real dual headlamps, a move that necessitated getting approval from each of the forty-eight states. Eight states failed to ratify the change in time, causing Plymouth to mount a parking lamp inboard of each single headlamp.

A massive front bumper split the grille into two parts, the bumper bar rising up slightly as it crossed the middle of the car, giving a slight barbell shape to the grille. Above the bumper sat the regular grille of thin horizontal bars adorned with a rather abstract version of the Mayflower ship. Under the center part of the bumper was an ungainly looking vertically slotted underpan. If there was an Achilles heel in the Plymouth design it was this underpan; dealers and customers alike complained, and by mid-January the pan, originally sporting six vertical slots, was changed, dividing each slot with a thin vertical bar. An optional bumper guard also helped hide the offending pan.

It was at the rear of the car that Flite Sweep styling really came into its own. Taillamp lenses completely filled the slightly canted, finned rear fenders–between the lamps was a large expanse of smooth deck lid broken only by the deck lid ornament. Once again the name Plymouth would only appear at the front of the car. Round backup lights again sat below the taillamps reminiscent of the 1956 "jet pod's." Rear bumper underpans swept up from beneath a split-level rear bumper that repeated, much more smoothly, the design of the front bumper. The center of the rear bumper was grooved, with a chrome extension cascading down over the rear body pans.

Side trim was kept to a minimum. Model names appeared on the rear fenders, a "V" on the front fender signified V-8 power. Even the hubcaps were smooth, coming to a peak at the center. These hubcaps would prove to be popular with the custom car crowd and saw use on many other makes than Plymouth. Belvedere models were generally adorned with a single spear of stainless running from the front fender's tip to the rear of the car. A double set of spears provided a wedge for color

The 1957 Fury sported dual four-barrel carburetors. As in 1956, the exterior was finished in white with gold anodized side trim. Owner: Paul Blausey.

A most unusual accessory was the Hiway Hi-Fi which was connected through the radio to the speakers. Records ran at an extremely slow speed. Despite being offered through 1960, few Hiway Hi-Fi units were sold; today it's a much sought-after accessory. *Monte McElroy*

contrasts that were usually painted the same color as the roof in two-tone applications. Savoys had to settle for a stainless strip beginning at the forward point of the front door, running back to a level point with the rear bumper. On two-tone applications, a canted strip of stainless fell back from this horizontal molding to the rocker panel midway on the front door. The lower body area was painted to match the roof color in two-tone applications. The Plaza, reflecting its low-level status, was usually found without any body side moldings, although the Savoy trim could be added for two toning. Likewise, station wagons followed the same patterns as the car lines, the Sport Suburban getting Belvedere trim, the Custom Suburban Savoy trim, and the Deluxe no trim.

There was more to the new Plymouth than just style. Engineering had been busy as well, dropping the old independent coil-spring front suspension in favor of a torsion bar setup with ball-joint steering. Torsion bars were not new (Packard had a complex four-wheel torsion bar setup in 1955 and 1956), but the Chrysler switch to the torsion system marked a first for a major American manufacturer. With its new Torsion-Aire Ride (there was no air in the system, but with GM and others ready to launch true air-bag suspensions it was obligatory to include the word "Aire"), Plymouth (and its Chrysler stable mates) became the best handling cars on the American roadways. Racer Brown, writing in the May 1957 issue of *Hot Rod* magazine, said, "There is no question at least in my mind, that the weight distri-

bution of the Plymouth has a very great deal to do with the manner in which the car handles. The distribution figures closely approach some theoretical ideals of sports cars, but set a new standard for full-sized American passenger cars. After thoroughly wringing out the standard Plymouth on all types of road and under nearly every conceivable condition, I was ready to take on all comers and prove the Plymouth was the most roadable passenger car ever built in this country." *Motor Trend* went one step further and named Plymouth the best handling car in the country–eventually awarding the 1957 *Motor Trend* Car Of The Year Award to Chrysler Corporation's five divisions based on "Superior Handling and Roadability Qualities."

Torsion-Aire Ride was the combination of several re-engineered components, including the frame, wheels and tires, suspension, and steering linkage. Torsion-Aire incorporated two chrome steel bars mounted parallel to the inner walls of the front frame rails. The front portion of the bar was mounted to the lower control arms while the opposite end was anchored to the car's frame. As the suspension moved up and down the bars twisted, providing springing action.

Plymouth's superb handling also owed much to the redesigned rear leaf springs. Called "Levelizer springs" they were designed with short, stiff leaves in front of the axle and long, soft leaves at the rear. The rear axle was also moved forward of center. This arrangement controlled rear-end "squat" under acceleration. Changing from the splay mounting used since 1953, the springs were now outboard of the frame at both the front and rear of the spring. This helped lower the car's center of gravity and improve rear stability. All models received four springs per side with the exception of heavy-duty suspensions and Suburbans, which had six leaves.

Plymouth brakes, which had always been a strong point, were redesigned and increased to 11in on all models (12in late in the year on police cars). Called "Total Contact" braking, a full floating shoe contacted the drum along its length and width for greater braking power. The shoe moved between two rigid steel center plane support plates to guide it evenly to the drum and prevent the twisting found in ordinary brakes. The flexible shoes conformed to the drum even if the drum was temporarily distorted by hard braking. Plymouth continued to be the only car in the low-priced field with two brake cylinders on the front brakes.

As was the practice, Plymouths were model coded based on status and engine. Six-cylinder Plymouths were coded P30, the V-8 cars P31. Again a numerical designation indicated the series, 1 being a Plaza, 2 a Savoy, and 3 a Belvedere.

Belvedere buyers had their choice between a club sedan (two door), four-door sedan, Sport

Coupe (two-door hardtop), Sport Sedan (four-door hardtop), and a convertible, all with a choice of 6- or 8-cylinder power except for the convertible, which mandated a V-8.

Savoy buyers found one more model to choose from in 1957 with the addition of a Sport Sedan four-door hardtop, which joined the more familiar offerings of a club sedan, four-door sedan, and two-door hardtop Sport Coupe. Plaza buyers were still given three choices, a four-door sedan, club sedan, and the club sedan-based business coupe. True to tradition, the Plaza business coupe saw the least production of any 1957 Plymouth.

Station wagon buyers continued to be a growing segment of the market (14 percent of Plymouth's 1957 production), and Plymouth gave these buyers just what they wanted in the form of six different models. At the top of the line was the four-door Sport Suburban, available with either six- or nine-passenger seating. The four-door Custom Suburban could also be had with six- or nine-pas-

senger seating, while the two-door Custom Suburban and Deluxe Suburban offered only six-passenger seating.

The Fury didn't make its public debut until December 3, 1956. Like the first Fury, the car was designed as a high-performance, personal luxury car much in the vein of the Chrysler 300s and was available only in egg-shell white with gold accents. Interior appointments included an exclusive combination of cocoa and beige vinyl with coarse, woven cloth inserts; chrome moldings; a 150mph speedometer; special steering wheel; two interior dome lights; glovebox lock; safety padding package; and airfoam seat cushions.

Under the hood was Plymouth's most potent powerplant ever, a 290hp 318ci engine pumping 9.25:1 compression fed by dual Carter carburetors. Spent gasses flowed out low-restriction dual exhausts. Helping get the power to the road was a complement of heavy-duty equipment, including a 10-1/2in clutch plate for standard-equipped cars,

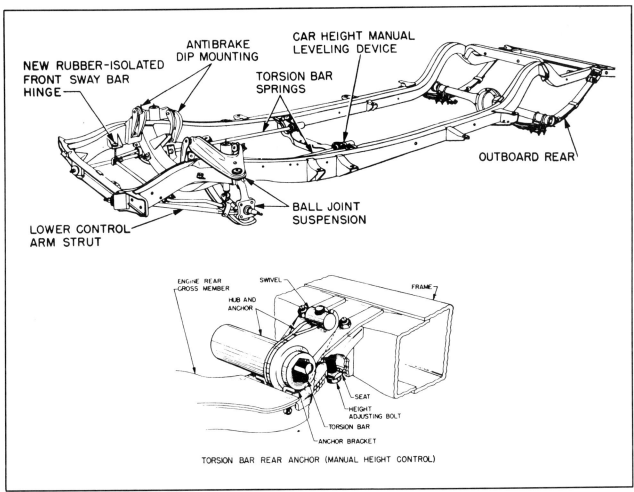

TORSION BAR REAR ANCHOR (MANUAL HEIGHT CONTROL)

"Torsion-Aire" suspension had nothing to do with true air suspension. Torsion bars replaced regular coil springs and could be adjusted to change the car's ride height. Torsion bars plus ball joint suspension made Plymouth the best handling car on the road in 1957.

Pillarless Belvedere hardtop sedan gracefully carried the new styling into a four-door body. Owner: Brian MacKay.

Dual air cleaners running to each side of the engine were used only in 1957. The air cleaners moved to the top of the carbs for 1958. *Jim Benjaminson*

heavy-duty shocks, heavy-duty 120lb-in rear springs, and special 8.00x14in nylon black sidewall tires mounted on 6in rims. Chrysler's new three-speed TorqueFlite automatic was also available. Chrysler may have fallen to the back of the pack before it finally offered a fully automatic transmission, but once in the fray, nothing held them back. Derived from the two-speed PowerFlite, the three-speed TorqueFlite would go on to fame and glory. During the drag racing wars of the early 1960s many racers were astounded to find MoPar drivers using an automatic, rather than the obligatory four-on-the-floor. Coupled to the Fury's dual quad 318, TorqueFlite proved to be a popular option.

TorqueFlite was optional on all P31-3 models and could be had on P31-2 or P31-3 cars if they were equipped with the optional V-800 engine. PowerFlite remained on the option list for all P30 and P31 models except those with the V-800 option (the V-800 option came on line one week after introduction of the Fury, essentially providing Fury power for any Plymouth body style). By the end of the year, Plymouth had sold a higher percentage of cars equipped with automatics than either of its two low-priced competitors.

V-8 buyers (Plymouth would also sell a higher percentage of V-8 cars in 1957 than Chevrolet or Ford) could choose between the 277ci engine, which now developed 197hp, an additional 10hp over 1956 thanks to a different camshaft and carburetor, or the Fury 301. The 277 was available only in the Plaza. The Fury 301 was the standard V-8 in Belvederes and Savoys and optional in the Plaza. Looking much like the later 318s, the 301 made a one-year-only appearance in 1957. The 301 was based on the 318 block , but had the same 3-1/8in stroke as the 277 (the 301's bore was bigger, though). Like the Plaza's 277, the 301 could be had with dual exhaust. Pumping out 215hp in standard form, an additional $36.20 would add a Fury 301 Quad package consisting of a four-barrel carburetor, special distributor, and dual exhausts, raising horsepower to 235 at 4400rpm. Adding some confusion to this engine was the use of the term "Fury." The Fury 301 V-8 could be had in all car lines except the Fury itself, which came with the 318 as its only powerplant.

The Fury V-800 engine option, which could be had in any body style, added $245 to the price of the car. Unlike "power packages" offered by Chevrolet, Ford, or even Dodge, the buyer got more

This Savoy four-door is powered by a V-8 as evidenced by the front fender emblem. Owner: David Fomasi.

115

Capturing top honors in the 1957 Mobil Gas Economy Run was this Belvedere Sport Sedan driven by Mary Davis. She would compete again the next year but had to settle for second place behind another Plymouth.

than just a hot engine; the package including a heavy-duty transmission (either manual or Torque-Flite), heavy-duty torsion bars, springs, shocks, and 14x6in wheels. Plymouth also offered an "uninstalled engine high-performance package" for 277 and 303 engines–what some considered to be an update for last year's Fury. Retailing for $243.45, this package included a dual-quad intake manifold with carburetors, linkage, air cleaners, special tappets and camshaft, gaskets, and a hand choke.

For fleet buyers or the staid set, the old, reliable 6-cylinder soldiered on. A slight boost in power to 132hp at 3600rpm was achieved through an increased compression ratio of 8:1. The 6-cylinder power pack was discontinued. Sixes could be had in any model except the Fury and Belvedere convertible and proved to be popular with taxi cab buyers. Sixes in taxis ran an 8.2:1 compression ratio using a special cylinder head (part 1821845 with casting 1821682–the standard head had part 1731545 with casting 1676337).

Standard axle ratios for 6-cylinder cars at the beginning of the year were 3.73 for manual transmissions (4.1 in mountain areas), 4.1 with overdrive, and 3.73 with PowerFlite (3.9 in mountain areas). V-8s came with 3.54 on standard shift cars, 3.9 for mountain driving and overdrive cars, 3.54 for PowerFlite (3.73 in mountains), and 3.36 with TorqueFlite. Beginning with cars built after February 15, these ratios were changed to 3.36 for PowerFlite V-8s and to 3.18 for TorqueFlite V-8s. A 2.93 axle was offered as an option for TorqueFlite cars beginning in May. The 3.36 ratio was dropped entirely at the end of June, being replaced by a 3.31 ratio.

As Plymouth's reputation for building hot cars grew, it would only seem logical that gas mileage would take a back seat to performance. Still, Mary Davis, driving an 8-cylinder Belvedere Sport Sedan

Door panel trim—Fury on the left, Belvedere on the right. *Monte McElroy*

in the 1957 Mobil Gas Economy Run, proved Plymouth could hold its own. Her car, with a 3.18 axle ratio and 200 "break in" miles on it, scored a first-place in the low-price field, with a winning average of 21.3907mpg. A second V-8 Belvedere, driven by Richard Griffith, attained a reading of 20.8968mpg.

Air conditioning continued to grow in popularity. For the first time, all system components were moved under the hood and incorporated into the heating unit, making more room in the trunk where previous components had lived. Hiway Hi-Fi continued as a rarely seen option, as was the Benrus steering wheel watch which incorporated a clock in the center hub of the steering wheel.

A "Flight Type" instrument panel placed all instruments and controls within reach of the driver. The speedometer, fuel and temp gauges, oil pressure, and amp warning lights (and an optional clock) were mounted in an oval pod on top of the dash panel. Push-button controls for the automatic transmission continued to reside on the driver's left side. Another of the Plymouth Achilles Heel design features was the interior rear-view mirror mounted to the forward windshield molding atop the dash. Why anyone thought this was a better place than hanging from the upper windshield molding remains a mystery.

Belvedere interiors offered five choices of Flite Wave cloth and vinyl along with bright gold or silver mylar inserts on door panels. Belvedere convertibles were available with standard Belvedere coupe interiors of five two-tone vinyl designs. Tops continued to be available in black, white, blue, or green. Savoy models could be ordered in any of four Mosaic Weave cloths and vinyl combos while the Plaza limited buyers to three colors of Fleck Cord and vinyl. Sport Suburban interiors were available in three combinations of Sport Tweed cloth and vinyl, while the Custom Suburban (a mid-class vehicle) offered four of the five all-vinyl interior combinations offered on the Belvedere convertible! Deluxe Suburbans offered a single interior choice—white Velva-Grain and tan Linen-Texture vinyl. Sport Coupes, Sport Sedans, and Suburbans used multi-piece headliners of pressed board, the sedan models using three pieces per vehicle, Suburbans six. Originally offered in white, blue, or green, the latter two colors were discontinued when supplies ran out in May, leaving white headliners as standard for all three body styles.

The year 1957 would prove to be Plymouth's best ever, bettering the 1955 record by more than 60,000 cars. Detroit, Evansville, Los Angeles, Windsor, and a new (April 1957) plant at Newark, Delaware, churned out 762,231 cars for a market that just couldn't get enough 1957 Plymouths. In the process Plymouth marched smartly ahead of Buick, reclaiming its traditional third place. Plymouth accounted for over half of Chrysler Corpora-

This Savoy club sedan has an amazing 20mi on the speedometer. Owner: Richard Pomroy.

tion's 1957 sales, as the corporation grabbed 20.4 percent of the market—the 10 millionth Plymouth rolled off the lines January 24, 1957. Reports of Los Angeles Ford and Chevy dealers discounting cars up to 15 percent to get customers into showrooms were commonplace—still there was no way Plymouth could compete head-to-head with production from either Ford or Chevrolet. And for the first time since 1935 Ford would find itself the number-one seller with final registrations of 1,493,617 cars. The 1957 Chevrolet, so highly revered in today's collector market, found itself bumped to second place. Chrysler had spent $300 million to bring the 1957 models to light, but in the long run they paid a terrible price for their victory.

The cars, without a doubt, were some of the best designs turned out by Virgil Exner and his stylists. If they had truly been intended as 1960 models, they hit the showrooms without a full complement of testing. This, combined with breakneck schedules to meet demands, saw quality control take a horrendous slide. The cars leaked dust and rain water like a sieve, paint faded and flaked off in chunks, and upholstery materials disintegrated in the sunlight. To find a Plymouth (or other Chrysler product) without a tear in the seam of the driver's seat became a near impossibility. Plymouth's highly touted torsion bar suspension wasn't without its share of troubles—a rubber boot originally intended to keep dirt and moisture out of the hex end of the bar had been deleted by "bean counters." As moisture, dirt, and rust began to build up, the bars began to bind and then snap, sending the car nose-diving to the broken side. Fortunately this usually hap-

The Buried Belvedere

"This is the sort of thing that could happen only in Tulsa," spoke Lewis Roberts Jr. during dedication ceremonies marking the observance of Tulsa's Golden Jubilee Week. "Tulsarama!" chairman Roberts' made his remarks as citizens prepared to entomb a new 1957 Plymouth Belvedere sport coupe as part of a time capsule buried on the southeast corner of the Tulsa County Courthouse lawn.

Why would anyone want to bury a new car? Roberts was asked. "The 'Tulsarama!' committee," he replied, "decided on the event after looking for a method of acquainting the citizens of the twenty-first century with a suitable representation of 1957 civilization."

"In our judgment," commented W.A. Anderson, Jubilee chairman, "Plymouth is a true representative of automobiles of this century—with the kind of lasting appeal that should still be in style fifty years from now. . . . Tulsans think big. And we feel we can overcome any technical difficulties we encounter [burying the Plymouth] including the possibility of striking oil in our excavation!"

Supplied through the cooperation of the Plymouth Division of Chrysler and Tulsa Plymouth dealers Wilkerson Motor Company, Cox Motor Company, Vance Motor Company, Forster Riggs and Parrish-Clark, the Belvedere has remained buried since June 15, 1957.

As part of the "Tulsarama!" festivities, citizens of Tulsa were asked to guess what the population of Tulsa would be in the year 2007. The guesses were then recorded on microfilm and sealed in a steel container buried with the car. When the car and artifacts are excavated, the person whose guess is closest to Tulsa's 2007 population is to be awarded the Belvedere. If that person is dead, the car is to be awarded to his or her heirs.

And what, exactly, will the lucky winner get when the car is unearthed in 2007? No one is really sure. Sitting on a steel skid, the white and gold car was wrapped in a cosmoline-like substance to help preserve it and then buried within a concrete bunker. (The car was lowered into the vault several times prior to June 15 for photo shoots, one such photo appearing on page twenty-five of *Life* magazine's July 7 issue.) Twenty years after the car's burial, questions were raised as officials began to wonder if the vault would maintain its integrity for fifty years. Its location (marked by a bronze plaque on the courthouse lawn) places it close to modern traffic. Buck Rudd, deputy chief of building operations for the county courthouse, mused in 1987, "There's a lot of traffic going by only 15 or 20ft from that thing. We've been curious to know if vibrations from the heavy traffic might have caused it to crack. "If moisture starts getting in there, it's going to cause things to deteriorate over fifty years time," Rudd continued. Unknown to the committee—or anyone else then—1957 Plymouths were terribly prone to rust. Asked what type of maintenance was done on the time capsule, Rudd replied, "We just cut the grass on top of it."

While some lucky person may (or may not) win a brand-new 1957 Plymouth in the year 2007, the winner has several other prizes to look forward to, among them a $100 trust fund accruing interest until the year 2007. Included with the Plymouth is a 5gal can of gasoline, a jar of Oklahoma crude oil, and in the glovebox fourteen bobby pins, a ladies' compact, plastic rain cap, several combs, a tube of lipstick, pack of gum, facial tissues, $2.73 in bills and coins and a pack of cigarettes with matches—all items that might have been found in a woman's purse circa 1957.

The car's glove compartment contains two other interesting items: a parking ticket (unpaid!) and a bottle of tranquilizers. Depending on the Belvedere's condition, the tranquilizers may be the most important part of the package.

The lucky person who in 1957 correctly guessed what Tulsa, Oklahoma's population would be in 2007 is destined to win the brand-new 1957 Belvedere Sport Coupe sealed in a time capsule beneath Tulsa's courthouse. *Chrysler Historical Foundation*

pened at slow speeds. The rubber boot was quickly resurrected, but not without cost to Chrysler's reputation.

Quality control was little more than a laughing matter around Detroit in 1957; after all, they were selling cars as fast as they could build them. With 1957 sales reaching 6.1 million cars, Detroit was equally content to shrug off reports that 1957 marked the first year the U.S. imported more automobiles (259,343) than it exported (141,381). The foreign invasion had begun and in the long run the American automobile industry would pay dearly for its mistakes.

Despite its killer good looks, the 1957 Plymouth—and its stable mates—gave Chrysler Corporation a long standing reputation for poor quality. Dave Holls' words ring true, again commenting in *Collectible Automobile*, "The biggest problem is that they [the 1957 Plymouths] were the worst cars Chrysler ever made. Quality was terrible, so every car they sold made an enemy instead of a friend." It was an image still haunting the corporation as late as 1980 when Lee Iacocca went before the U.S. Congress to plead for a billion dollar loan to keep Chrysler Corporation alive.

In the boardroom an important but unheralded program to establish single-line Plymouth dealerships was being undertaken; during the year 200 "exclusive" dealerships free of Chrysler, Dodge, or DeSoto influence were set up with more expected in 1958. For the next few years Plymouth would find itself on a roller coaster ride of corporate changes. Recognizing the need to modernize, plans were made to phase out Evansville as soon as a new plant near St. Louis, Missouri, could be completed. The St. Louis plant, covering 1.3 million square feet of floor space, would service 1,400 dealerships in the southern U.S.

1958: More Of The Same

Hungrily looking forward to another year as good as the last one, Plymouth dealers gazed upon a car that at first glance had few, if any, changes. Like the 1950 compared to the 1949, it was easy to assume there were few differences between the two cars. In its December 1957 issue, *Motor Life* commented, "If any could get by in 1958 without a major change, that car would be Plymouth."

In an era when change for the sake of change was prevalent, there were gripes from some dealers that the cars hadn't changed enough. Often when a stunning design is introduced the next year's remake spoils the original—not so with the 1958 Plymouth. What few changes were made were mostly for the better. Unfortunately for the industry—and the country—the nation was gripped by a short economic downturn since labeled the "Eisenhower recession." Sales for the first half of 1958 were the lowest since 1952, year-end totals nosediving from

Dart-shaped design was best exemplified by the Belvedere convertible. Owner: Monte McElroy.

6,113,000 cars in 1957 to 4,258,000 for calendar year 1958. Chevrolet sales had managed to pick up by 2.2 percent based largely on Chevy's all-new car. Plymouth sales dropped 1.6 percent, while Ford sank 2.9 percent. Chrysler corporate sales were off by 47 percent. Plymouth managed to hold onto the third-place sales ranking it had fought so hard to gain back in 1957. Buick was having its own troubles, reeling from the unpopular styling of its 1957 cars. For 1958, Plymouth's challenge would come from Rambler.

Two of 1957's most criticized features were changed for the better. The lower bumper pan was replaced by a lower grille that matched the upper section in an opening reminiscent of the Chrysler 300 grille. The other change came in the form of real dual headlamps, which had now been legalized in all forty-eight states. Adding the second sealed beam meant Plymouth had to find somewhere else to mount the parking lamps, which they cleverly nestled under the headlight brow above the twin lamps. On the edge of the hood rode a winged ornament with "Plymouth" embedded in it while the grille had a prominent "V" ornament (V-8 cars only). For the first time since 1928 the Mayflower did not appear anywhere on the car.

Market Share - (Calendar Year 1958)
    Chevrolet–26.5 percent
    Ford–22.1 percent
    Plymouth–8.4 percent

The Fury was still Plymouth's factory hot rod. In 1958, buyers had a choice of engines, either 318ci or 361ci, both with dual four-barrel carburetors. All 1958 Furys were painted Buckskin Beige. Gold anodized side trim remained an exclusive Fury feature. Owner: Dale McQuillin.

The "Silver Special" was based on the Plaza Club Sedan whose equipment included Sportone trim with silver paint in the insert and on the roof. The price in 1958 was $1,958. Owner: Martin Dole.

If there was a downfall to the 1958 design it was the taillights. The fin-filling lens of 1957 was replaced by a chrome spike (Plymouth called it a reflecting tower) that was supposed to reflect red from the taillight over the aluminum panel inside the fin blade, the taillight taking the place of the round back-up lamps of the year before. The back-up light, now a single unit, was built into the center of the rear bumper.

Belvederes all sported Fury-style side trim flowing from the front fender at an angle toward the rear of the car before kicking up to reach the tailfin's upper edge. Two-tone Sportone versions could have this area filled with silver anodized aluminum trim much like the gold trim used on the Fury, or the spear could be painted a contrasting color. Belvederes without Sportone trim had a single stainless spear running from front to rear in a straight line. These cars, when two toned, had the roof painted to contrast with the lower body.

The Savoy Sportone mimicked 1957 DeSoto trim, forming a forward-pointing arrow along the bottom of the body. Savoys without Sportone had the same horizontal stainless trim as the plain Belvederes. The Plaza, normally the plain Jane of the group, had an abbreviated stainless strip run-

Christine: Curse or Blessing?

Stephen King is noted as America's leading writer of horror stories. An automobile historian, he is not. Yet Stephen King has had a most profound effect on one automobile, the 1958 Plymouth Fury.

With the publication of his book *Christine* and subsequent John Carpenter movie by the same name, the 1958 Plymouth Fury has taken on cult status. When asked why he picked the 1958 Fury, King explained that he chose it because the car was "one good looking 1950s car that, unlike such cars as the

The Columbia Pictures movie, *Christine,* starred Keith Gordon as Arnie Cunningham, Alexandra Paul as Leigh Cabot, and John Stockwell as Dennis Guilder. Lurking in the background is the evil *Christine,* a "red and white Fury" in Stephen King's horror novel of the same name. *Columbia Pictures*

1949–51 Mercs or 1955–57 Chevys, didn't have a cult mythology built up around it."

Christine is the story of Arnie Cunningham, a high school outcast with a pizza pie complexion and with one true friend to his name, his buddy Dennis Guilder. One fateful afternoon Dennis is driving Arnie home from work when they pass a decrepit house with an equally decrepit 1958 Plymouth Fury sitting out back with a "for sale" sign on it. It's love at first sight for Arnie, although Dennis tries to talk him out of buying the car from an old soldier named Roland D. LeBay.

Arnie takes the car home, but his parents won't allow the wreck of a Fury to sit in their driveway. Arnie and the car, named Christine, end up at Will Darnell's garage and wrecking yard. Darnell, an unsavory character, allows Arnie to work on the Fury in exchange for Arnie performing illicit "errands" for him.

At this point Christine's evil begins working on Arnie; he has a falling out with his parents, his complexion clears up, and suddenly he's dating the most beautiful girl in school, Leigh Cabot. And Christine, formerly a candidate for the back row of any self-respecting junkyard, slowly revitalizes herself to the point where the Fury is showroom new.

When a group of bullies enter Arnie's life demolishing the car in revenge for Arnie getting them kicked out of school, Christine, protecting her owner, goes on a killing rampage.

The movie depicts Christine rejuvenating herself each time something happens. During the movie's filming nearly two dozen "Christines" were demolished to film the scenes. Cars reportedly restored at a cost of $10,000 each were systematically destroyed to make the movie—in total some $1.5 million was spent in restoring and demolishing 1958 Plymouths (Belvedere and Savoy hardtops, appropriately made up, were also part of the fleet.) To achieve the special effects of the car regenerating itself after a smash up, at least one car was crushed by hydraulic jacks mounted inside the car, which literally pulled the car in on itself. The film was run backward to give the illusion of the car restoring itself.

In making the movie, an abandoned furniture plant in Sun Valley, California, was converted to resemble the original Plymouth factory; the opening scenes of the movie accurately depicts rows of new 1958 Plymouths coming down an assembly line.

In the end Dennis and Leigh are responsible for seeing that Christine is destroyed. As the movie ads asked, "How do you kill something that can't possibly be alive?" Arnie, like Christine and her former owner Roland D. LeBay, doesn't survive.

Following release of the Columbia Pictures movie, 1958 Furys became hot property. Christine look-alikes began popping up around the country. Columbia gave away at least two Christines after the

The movie faithfully recreated the 1958 Plymouth assembly line. Here Christine comes "off the line." *Columbia Pictures*

The *Christine* plot called for several cars to be demolished during the course of filming—this scene brought tears to the eyes of many Plymouth fans. Christine got her revenge by killing each of her assailants. Movie posters asked, "How can you kill something that can't possibly be alive?" *Columbia Pictures*

Christine, the movie, spurred much interest in 1958 Plymouths. Many cars have been restored to look like the movie car, as evidenced by this car which bears personalized license plates reading, "EVIL 58." Owner: Vince McPhee.

film, and dozens of others have been restored in her honor. There was just one problem: Stephen King's version of the 1958 Plymouth Fury was totally inaccurate.

King's description of the car gave it a red and white paint scheme—all 1958 Furys were Buckskin Beige. When cornered on the question, King said the original owner had the car custom painted, but the movie version shows the car coming off the line red and white.

Several times in the book King refers to Christine as a four door—all Furys were two-door hardtops. Other little details showed King's lack of knowledge regarding 1958 Plymouths. In one passage Dennis tries to open Christine's door by jamming his "thumb down on the button below the handle"—a neat trick considering Plymouth didn't use push-button door handles until 1962. Several references are made to Christine's door lock buttons, and the movie depicts GM-style door lock knobs being sucked in by the evil Christine when she wants to trap someone inside. In reality, the front doors of 1958 Plymouths were locked by pushing forward on the door handle; rear doors used a small wing knob on the side panel.

King's underhood descriptions are equally laughable. At one point he calls the engine a 382 (did he mean 383?) then later corrects himself to a 318 with "speed lines on the air cleaner." The real Fury had two four-barrel carburetors, each with its own air cleaner. King calls the transmission a "hydramatic controlled by a gearshift lever which Leigh was afraid was going to pop out of park." Plymouths, of course, did not use Hydramatic (a GM term spelled with a capital "H"), the Fury had a TorqueFlite with no "park" position on the dash-mounted push buttons.

Adding insult to injury was the rear cover photo on the hard cover edition of the book, which found King sitting on the hood of a 1957 Plymouth, rather than a 1958 as featured in the book.

In the long run, the Christine phenomena has proven to be both a curse and a blessing for the 1958 Plymouth. The curse came in the large number of already rare 1958 Plymouths demolished in making the movie. The blessing has come in raising the profile of a car that might otherwise have remained ignored. Lanny Knutson, writing in the *Plymouth Bulletin*, observed, "Christine has likely given us more restored 1957–58 Plymouths that would otherwise have been left to rot. And, among the public, Christine has raised the profile of Plymouths to greater heights."

ning from the forward edge of the front door back to the bumper as standard (on later cars only) with an optional Sportone forming a spear covering the doors. When two toned, the roof and spear were painted colors that contrasted the body's.

Buyers were given their choice of a Belvedere Sport Coupe, Sport Sedan, four-door sedan, two-door club sedan, or convertible. Savoys offered the same line-up with the exception of the convertible; Plaza buyers were given just three models to chose from, a four-door sedan, two-door club sedan, and the rear-seatless two-door business coupe based on the club sedan body. As usual, an optional rear seat was available for the business coupe.

Station wagon buyers weren't overlooked, as wagon sales grew to 28.3 percent of production. At the top of the line was the Sport Suburban in either six- or nine-passenger form corresponding to the Belvedere, followed by the Custom Suburban (Savoy trim) four door in six- or nine-passenger format, and a Custom (Plaza) four-door six-passenger wagon. Two-door, six-passenger wagons could also be had in Custom or Deluxe trim. All models were available with choice of 6- or 8-cylinder power with the exception of the Belvedere convertible and Fury. Later in the model year it was announced that the Custom Suburban had become the first station wagon to ever lead body style sales in the Plymouth line. Before the end of the year, the Savoy four-door slipped past to edge the wagon out 67,933 to 61,790 for that honor.

In its final year as Plymouth's factory hot-rod, the Fury (advertised as the "Star Of The Forward Look") gave customers the choice of two V-8 engines–the standard 290hp Dual Fury V-800 318 or the new 305hp Golden Commando 350, both sporting dual four-barrel carburetors backed by a 10-1/2in heavy-duty clutch manual transmission or three-speed TorqueFlite automatic.

Getting power to the pavement fell to heavy-duty torsion bars, shock absorbers, and rear springs, and high-performance 8.00x14in nylon tires on 6in wide wheels.

Fury's trademark upswept side spear was shared with the Sportone Belvedere, the difference being that the Fury's trim was gold anodized. Other anodized gold trim included the grille and hubcap centers. Inside, a custom two-tone beige, cocoa, and gold interior replaced the previous gold on white. Sun visors and instrument panels were padded, and the speedometer topped at 150mph. New for the year was a switch to Buckskin Beige from the traditional egg-shell white of the 1956–1957 Fury.

Interior differences to the rest of the line were minimal, the most noticeable change coming in the movement of the rear-view mirror—still mounted on the dash panel but moved forward from the windshield molding. Belvedere four door and club sedan upholstery featured blue, green, coral, or black "Reflections"-pattern, metallic threaded Jacquard fabric with bolsters of dark blue, dark green, or black vinyl with the blue, green, or coral seats; white or red vinyl with black seats. Sport Coupes and Sport Sedans used blue, green, coral, or black "Calypso"-pattern, metallic threaded Jacquard fabric with white vinyl bolsters on all colors, with red bolsters available for black seats. Convertibles used blue, green, coral, or black "Wovenaire" ventilating vinyl with white vinyl bolsters, red again available on request with black seats.

Savoys were fitted with blue, green, or black "Star Cluster" Jacquard fabric with bolsters of blue or green with seats of the same color; white bolsters were used with black seats or red if requested regardless of body style. Plaza buyers had the choice of blue, green, or black "Textured Moderne" Jacquard with beige bolsters used on blue or green seats, black bolsters with black seats. Sport Suburbans got the Savoy "Calypso" interior pattern and colors, Custom Suburbans the convertible's "Wovenaire" vinyl in blue, green, or black, while Deluxe Suburbans came in a single shade of beige on black "Sequin" pattern ventilating vinyl with beige bolsters.

Few changes were made under the hood—the PowerFlow Six struggled on for one more year, developing 132hp at 3600rpm. The base V-8 was the Fury V-800, a 318ci 225hp two-barrel which was standard on all models except the Fury. Like its four-barrel cousin, the Fury V-800 with Super Pak (250hp) could be mated to the straight-stick trans-

mission (with or without overdrive), PowerFlite, or three-speed TorqueFlite. The Dual Fury V-800, also a 318 but with 9.25:1 compression and dual four-barrel carburetors, was exclusive to the Fury and could be mated only to the standard transmission without overdrive or TorqueFlite.

Making a one-year-only appearance was the Golden Commando 350. This dual-carbed, 10:1 compression ratio V-8 developed 305hp at 5000rpm, churning out 370lb-ft of torque at 3600rpm. Based on the Chrysler "B" block introduced in 1958, the engine would later be more familiar in its 383, 426, and 440 forms (in addition to the later 361 and 400 versions). The 350 shared the same transmission options as the Dual Fury V-800.

Last but not least among engine options was the "soon to be available on any Plymouth except station wagons" Golden Commando with fuel injection. This powerplant was cataloged in the dealer data book as a "limited-production, optional engine designed for and offered to a select group of high-performance enthusiasts who demand an engine that's truly out of the ordinary [mating] fuel injection with the most advanced high-performance engine available in its field." Designed and built by

The instrument panel of the 1958 was little changed from 1957 with the exception of moving the rear-view mirror closer to the dashboard's edge. Owner: Johan Veltmans.

Bendix, the "Electrojector" system proved to be more fancy than fact. Published specifications rated the fuel-injected Golden Commando at 315hp, with the same torque and compression as the standard Golden Commando.

Exactly where the trouble lay with the Bendix system is not known. As an attempt to catch Chevrolet and Pontiac's mechanical Rochester fuel injection systems, the Bendix system proved a failure, so much so that the few injected cars in public hands were recalled and the units removed.

A new performance option for 1958 was the "Sure-Grip" differential. Sure-Grip prevented the momentary spinning of the wheels when poor traction was encountered. With the high-performance cars it also assured equal traction in getting the power to the roadway. Sure-Grip could be ordered with any engine from the six to the Golden Commando and with any transmission combination except overdrive. When coupled to the six with either standard or PowerFlite, the rear axle ratio was 3.73; 318s with stick or PowerFlite also got the 3.73 ratio, but with TorqueFlite the standard ratio was 3.31 although 3.73 could be ordered. The Golden Commando with manual transmission also used the 3.73 ratio, but TorqueFlite's standard ratio was 3.31 with the option of 3.73. Cars built after mid-May with Golden Commando and standard trans-mission had the ratio changed from 3.73 to 3.31 across the board.

Cars built with standard transmissions after February 21 received an all-new transmission providing more positive detent feel, shorter shift lever travel, and different ratios. The transmission housing, shift rods, and levers were also changed and did not interchange with earlier transmissions. These new transmissions were stamped with identifying letters: code letters LA for use on standard 6-cylinder cars, LB on 8-cylinder cars, LC for 6-cylinder cars with heavy-duty transmission, and LD for both 6- and 8-cylinder overdrive cars.

Motor Trend and *Motor Life* both road tested several 1958 Plymouths, *Motor Trend* pitting a Fury against an Impala and Fairlane 500 and later testing a Belvedere Sport Sedan (both Plymouths had the 305hp Golden Commando engine). *Motor Trend* also briefly drove a Savoy while *Motor Life* tested both a Belvedere Sport Sedan and a 6-cylinder, overdrive-equipped Savoy Club Sedan. In *Motor Trend*'s three-way comparison, Plymouth picked up "poorest front seat" honors. All three cars received bad marks for rear-seat entry and egress. Plymouth was easily picked as the best handling but with the harshest ride. Considering the Fury had a heavy-duty suspension, this was not surprising. All the Plymouths tested by both magazines

Belvederes used the same side trim as the 1957 Fury. The most noticeable change at the rear of the 1958 were the small, round taillamps. This car sports an unusual continental kit and fender skirts. Owner: Jan Stanggren.

walked away with top handling honors though all noted the cars had a tendency to wander when buffeted by side winds. Plymouth's three and a half turn lock-to-lock steering gave it the ease of handling award compared to Ford's four and a half and Chevrolet's five turns. Other accolades included good assembly and finish, good cornering and the "finest brakes in the industry." Road testers, however, faulted the TorqueFlite transmission calling it too "sensitive," preferring instead the smoothness of PowerFlite.

Performance comparisons of the three cars varied–the Chevrolet had a 280hp V-8, the Ford a 300hp and the Fury a 305hp. Overall gas mileage in stop-and-go driving gave Chevrolet top honors at 12.7mpg, with Ford in second at 10.3. The Fury returned a dismal 8.4mph. Highway driving brought similar results–Chevrolet 14.6mpg, Ford 13.4mpg and Plymouth 10.6mpg. Zero to 60mph tests showed Plymouth at its best, the Fury zipping to a 7.7sec run, followed by the Chevrolet in 9.1sec, with Ford bringing up the rear in 10.2sec. Quarter-mile times were much closer–while the Ford wasn't recorded in this test, Plymouth barely nipped out Chevrolet, reaching 86.5mph in 16.1sec to the Impala's 83.5mph in 16.5sec.

Nearly all of the road tests were conducted with the biggest V-8s, except for a July 1958 *Motor Life* road test of a 6-cylinder overdrive Savoy Club Sedan. *Motor Life*'s comments on the car were "good basic transportation" with a "marked air of austerity." The Savoy six recorded an overall average of 18mpg and lumbered through the 0–60mph trial in 16.2sec. Commenting on the car, *Motor Life* concluded, "Owning a Plymouth six instead of a V-8 unquestionably will result in saving some money in purchase price (the V-8 cost an additional $107) and operating and maintenance costs but the difference is so slight it will be worthwhile to only a few." Echoing the other magazines, *Motor Life* called the Plymouth's handling "magnificent." Road testers' preference for the V-8 echoed the buying public's–the Mound Road engine plant celebrated building its one millionth V-8 engine June 8.

Motor Trend's gas mileage results in comparing the Fury against an Impala and Fairlane 500 didn't reflect the mileage most people could expect from a Plymouth. For the second straight year, Plymouth captured the two top places for low-priced cars in the Mobilgas Economy Run. Mary Davis, who the year before had taken top honors, had to settle for second place behind Pierce Venable–his car averaging 20.0088mpg to Davis' 19.9897. Two cars scored higher mileages–one a Ford six, the other a Chevrolet six, but Venable's 48.3264ton/mpg was the determining factor in being declared overall winner. Davis' car turned in a 48.1801ton/mpg rating.

A new code system was introduced with the 1958 models , replacing the familiar "P" numbering system. Unknown to the general public the system had gone into effect years earlier, assigning a specific letter code to certain model years, presumably so competitors wouldn't know exactly what model year was being referred to should they hear of a development for a certain series of cars. The first cars to receive the code were the 1949 models, coded "C." Corresponding letters progressed through the years, skipping the letter "I," making the 1956 cars the "J" series. Hence 1958's new code system began with the letter "L," followed by "P" for Plymouth. Number codes were used to designate engines–"1" for 6-cylinder, "2" for V-8 cars. Following these letters and numbers was another letter designating price class–"L" for low prices, "M" for medium priced and "H" for high priced.

The lowest priced Plaza series became an LP1-L (six) or LP2-L (eight). Savoys were LP1-M or LP2-M and Belvederes LP1-H or LP2-H. The Fury used the V-8 Belvedere designation of LP2-H. In succeeding years, the first letter would move one step up the alphabet, the 1959s becoming the M series cars.

The code letters L, M, and H were used internally and did not appear in the cars' serial numbering system, which was also changed to reflect the new model codes. Under the new system serial numbers began with the first two code letters–L for 1958, P for Plymouth, followed by numbers "1" or "2" to designate 6- or 8-cylinder power. Serial numbers for all series began at 1001 and worked their way up. To designate which assembly plant the vehicle had been built in another code letter was added behind the model designation–except on

Plymouth police packages were becoming more popular. This Belvedere Club Sedan saw service with the East Hartford, Connecticut, Police Department. *East Hartford PD via Michael Morelli*

The owner of this 1958 Fury modified a Red Fish boat to match his car. Changes to the boat included the addition of Fury side trim and taillights. The trailer sports Fury turbine blade hubcaps.

Naturally, the boat is powered by a Chrysler outboard. Owner: Tom Mitchell. *Lanny Knutson.*

Detroit-built cars. Thus a 6-cylinder car built at Detroit would read LP1-1001, while a similar car built in Evansville had a serial number of LP1E-1001. These code letters were simple enough–E for Evansville, L for Los Angeles, N for Newark, Delaware, and W for Windsor, Ontario.

Midway through the model year a "Silver Special" package was introduced on Plaza two- and four-door sedans. Consisting of Sportone trim with anodized aluminum insert, front fender and door moldings, special metallic silver roof paint, full wheel covers, whitewall tires, directional signals, electric wipers, windshield washers, and "Forward Look" emblems pirated from the 1956 Plymouth, the two-door Silver Special was to sell for $1,958 in 1958. Another mid-year addition was the four-door Deluxe Suburban six-passenger wagon

There were also mid-year changes to the front pans located between the body and bumper, as noted by Chrysler stylist Jeff Godshall in a 1988 *Plymouth Bulletin*, "According to sales catalogs, both upper and lower grille pans were originally painted body color. Apparently this caused a problem in the plants. When the 1957 Chrysler Corporation Annual Report was published on February 13, 1958, the Plymouths pictured had argent lower

grille pans instead of body color. But when a *Ross Roy Confidential Bulletin* was issued March 14, 1958, both the lower grille pan and the center upper grille pan were painted argent, although the upper grille pans beneath the headlights remained body color. This last paint scheme was identical to that used on the 1957 Plymouth. This was probably the easiest to paint in the plants, since the grille pans were not part of the basic body and thus were a problem to paint body color. On both the 1957 and 1958 Furys, the upper and lower grille pans were painted the special Fury body color."

Despite reduced sales, Plymouth remained in third place. Virgil Exner, having returned to work after an illness (when he took ill in 1957 it was feared he would have to retire permanently) would be called on to redesign the 1957 bodies one more time.

1959: The End Of An Era

Plymouth's thirtieth anniversary models sat on the edge of change. When the last of these cars came off the assembly lines, the end of an era had been reached. The cars replacing them would be radically different, both in their mechanical attributes and the way they were built. The year 1959 would see the closing of one plant and the opening of another, and sadly, Plymouth would bid a long farewell to its coveted number-three spot on the sales charts.

Plymouth's competition entered the market year with completely new cars. The Ford had a more traditional look. Chevrolet–indeed, all of General Motors–had been so taken aback by Chrysler Corporation's 1957 models that a whole new series of cars had been ordered for 1959, despite the fact GM cars had been all new in 1958.

General Motors took a page from Chrysler in designing all of its 1959 bodies around one shell (Chrysler built all of its 1957 wagons on one shell). Chevrolet's entry was a wild-looking, bat-winged affair with huge horizontal tear drop taillights. As rumors floated in the trade press that Chrysler would soon go to unit body construction, Plymouth, in the last year of its three-year styling cycle, would have to make due with the 1957 body shell one more year. To combat the competition's all-new cars, Exner's redesign would have to be more radical than 1958's had been. The cost of retooling the 1959s ran $150 million, with most of that directed at Plymouth.

The restyling included a new anodized aluminum egg-crate grille with wrap-around parking/turn signal lamps, split by a black screen in the center where the Mayflower sailing ship once again made its appearance. This time the ship shared space with an upward pointing arrow (half of the former horizontal Forward Look emblem). And for the first time since 1928, the ship was seen from the front rather than from the back. Factory literature proclaimed "Plymouth's bright new emblem symbolizes the spirit in which the 1959 models have been created. A stylized representation of the Mayflower reflects Plymouth's great tradition. The missile poised above it portrays the pace-setting styling and engineering features that set Plymouth ahead in the new Space Age." Perhaps some of Chrysler's space program people had a hand in writing the prose? For Plymouth traditionalists, the good ship Mayflower sailed off into the sunset.

"Double-barreled" fenders drew attention to the sculpted eyebrows and floating dual headlamps. Taking a styling cue from the 1942 Plymouth's under-bumper air scoop, the 1959 version was designed to give a "jet-intake effect" (1942's had been inspired by race cars). The area beneath the bumper and stone shield were void of any grille

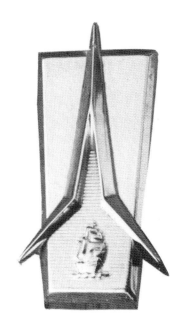

Making its last appearance on a Plymouth was the Mayflower, which was now combined with a rocket ship. For the first time since 1928, the ship was seen from the front, rather than from the rear. *Lanny Knutson.*

work. Fins began to rise at the "C" pillar in a smoother upsweep than previous years, lending the car's rear an illusion of greater length than there actually was. The fin was capped by fluted stainless trim, which cascaded down the fin to the deck lid.

The hood and deck lid were sculpted, the hood receiving a center windsplit, the deck lid cut from rear window to the body crease molding. This body crease was adorned with stainless trim on Fury and Sport Fury models. Back-up lamps moved back to the taillight in an oval cluster, rear bumpers indented in the middle to frame the license plate. Sportone trim was changed slightly and came standard on the Sport Fury and optional on other models. All Sportone panels featured inserts of textured anodized aluminum. A new Plymouth monogram rode on the left corner of the hood and deck lid, with model names in the same style script appearing at the rear edge of the fin.

Plymouth revamped its model names for 1959, dropping the price leader Plaza series. Taking its place was the Savoy in three body styles–four door, two door, and business coupe. One step above the Savoy was the equally demoted Belvedere series, offering a two door, four door, two-door hardtop, four-door hardtop, and convertible.

Taking the Belvedere's place was the Fury, which now became a series of cars rather than just a high-performance specialty vehicle. Fury models included a four door, four-door hardtop, and two-door hardtop. At the top of the line was the Sport

Fury, which included two models, a convertible and a two-door hardtop. Nineteen-fifty-nine marked the first year Plymouth offered two convertibles.

Station wagons continued their familiar nameplates. Leading the group was the four-door Sport Suburban in either six- or nine-passenger form; next in line was the Custom Suburban four door in six- or nine-passenger configuration. A Custom Suburban was also offered with two-door, six-passenger seating. Rounding out the wagon lineup were the six-passenger Deluxe Suburbans with either two or four doors.

For the purist, an era ended when the Fury name was degraded to include a full range of body styles. In later years the Fury name would be diluted even further, models being assigned Fury I, Fury II and Fury III nomenclature depending on price status. Why Plymouth decided to downgrade the Fury name is unknown. According to Jeff Godshall, obscure corporate records show model names considered for 1959 were Savoy, Wilshire, Belvedere, and Fury. While the first Furys had been all-out performance cars, the car replacing it was a more docile, and it was hoped, more salable unit.

"Combining Ivy League smartness with Big Ten performance" was Plymouth's description of the Sport Fury series. Powered by the Fury V-800 with Super Pak, the Fury concept had been carried to two body styles, adding a convertible to the already familiar two-door hardtop. Sport Furys were easily distinguished by their special trim, which included a new rendition of the upswept spear used since 1956, only this time the end of the spear formed a cove where a special "Tiffany touch" medallion rode. This circular medallion was finished in black and gold with the grille ornament repeated in the center. A fake spare tire cover was bolted to the deck lid, and the medallion was repeated in the center "hubcap." The continental tire look was a favorite of Exner, but most detractors simply called it the "toilet seat."

It was under the hood where the biggest change could be seen between the old Fury and Sport Fury. Standard in each Sport Fury was the 260hp 318, still with high-performance carburetor, though now there was just one. A high-performance camshaft, low-restriction exhaust, high-performance intake manifold, and distributor rounded out the engine package. This same engine could be ordered for any car except the Savoy business coupe. Transmission choices ran to everything Plymouth offered, three-speed with or without overdrive, PowerFlite, or TorqueFlite. Optional (at extra cost) was the Golden Commando 395 "B" block V-8, which replaced last year's 350. With a slightly bigger bore (4.12in to 4.06in) and the same stroke

Virgil Exner favored "classic" touches in his designs—a favorite was the fake spare tire in the "Sport Deck" as seen on this Fury Sport Coupe. Detractors simply called it a toilet seat. Owner: James Covington.

(3.38in), displacement jumped slightly to 361ci. The new engine was rated at 305hp at 4600rpm, virtually the same rating as the 350. Both shared the same 10:1 compression ratio. Like the Fury V-800 engine, the 361 used just a single carburetor–the engine took its name from its stump-pulling torque–395lb-ft at 3000rpm.

Special features included a high-performance camshaft, high-performance dual breaker distributor, and high-performance intake manifold and carburetor. This engine, too, was available on all models except the Savoy business coupe but could be coupled only to the three-speed transmission without overdrive or TorqueFlite.

For those whose horsepower needs were more mundane, the standard V-8 was the 230hp 318 with two-barrel economy carburetor. Only two models were restricted from using this engine–the Sport Fury and the Savoy business coupe. Transmission options included the three-speed with or without overdrive, PowerFlite, or TorqueFlite. Fleet buyers or those bent on economy still had the choice of the tired but faithful PowerFlow six. The six hadn't changed any in the last few years, and even the ad writers stopped twisting the figures.

Horsepower was still 132 at 3600rpm. All the long-standing 6-cylinder attributes were still in place including four-ring pistons and hardened valve seat inserts. New for 1959 were heat-resistant exhaust valves. The six could be had in any Belvedere except the convertible, all Savoys, the Deluxe Suburban, and the four-door six-passenger Custom Suburban, coupled to the standard transmission with or without overdrive or PowerFlite.

Making it three wins in a row, an 8-cylinder Plymouth copped top honors in the 1959 Mobil Gas Economy Run, squeaking out 21.15mpg–bettering the mileage of a 6-cylinder Ford by nearly a full mile per gallon on the 1,899-mile trial from Los Angeles to Kansas City. An 8-cylinder Ford came in second with 19.67mpg, and Chevrolet picked up third with 19.26mpg.

Early in 1957 work had begun in the back rooms of Chrysler to prepare a compact car for future sale in the U.S. This project had resulted in several engine designs including both in-line six and V-6 configurations. The in-line six design was chosen May 1, 1958, for an engine displacing 170ci. Realizing the need to replace the outmoded six in full-size Plymouth and Dodge passenger cars, the

Four-door sedans competed with station wagons for top sales honors. Pictured here is a Belvedere four door. Owner: Lori Prorak.

The instrument panel was redesigned for 1959, placing transmission push buttons to the left and heater-defroster controls to the right.

Swivel front seats were standard equipment in Sport Furys. A novel idea, they never really caught on and disappeared a few years later. *George Dalinis.*

same group of engineers were asked to design a suitable larger displacement engine. What followed was the famous Slant Six engine.

When the last 1959 Plymouths came off the line, the old reliable flathead six was put out to pasture (it was still used through 1968 in some Dodge trucks). It had served long and faithfully, powering millions of Plymouths, Dodges, and small Dodge trucks for twenty-six years. Its replacement would last until 1992, finding its way into 12.5 million vehicles.

Chassis remained much the same as the 1957-58 cars except for the addition of "Constant Level" Torsion-Aire. Air suspension systems were big news in the industry, General Motors particularly pushing them. The GM system was complex and trouble prone, leaving many a motorist stranded when his air-suspended car sank to the ground. Acting on the same principle, but applied only to the rear of the car, Constant Level Torsion-Aire worked in conjunction with the five-leaf spring package. The system utilized an under-hood air compressor supplying high-pressure air to a reserve tank that distributed air to rubberized nylon air springs mounted between the body and rear leaf springs. A height control valve automatically charged the air springs with more air to raise the rear end of the vehicle whenever a load was applied, allowing the car to sit level at all times. In case of a system failure, the rear springs (lighter duty units than cars without Constant Level) would still allow the vehicle to be driven.

Interiors featured a "Jet-Age Control Center" instrument cluster featuring an aircraft-style housing and enough buttons to keep the most ardent button-pusher happy. To the left of the speedometer in an angled panel were the transmission controls—four buttons for PowerFlite, five for Torque-

Flite. To the right, were another five buttons to control the heater, defroster, and air conditioning. Gauges included fuel and temperature with red lights monitoring oil pressure and amperes. Every control except the radio sat directly in front of the driver and was within easy reach (only the clock could be considered to be out of the driver's normal range). Riding directly above the steering wheel was the Mayflower emblem. Dash panels were color keyed to the interior and finished in No-Glare Royalite. Safety padding was optional. A change appreciated by all drivers were the left and right turn signal indicators placed on either side of the speedometer in place of the single-light indicator used for nearly a decade.

Sport Fury interiors featured viscose metallic cloth in blue, green, brown, or red with bolsters of red and metallic-hued vinyl. Door panels were four toned with seat and bolster materials, ivory vinyl, and a carpeted base strip. The coupe's headliners were ivory hardboard, using a perforated center section, scored side sections separated by ivory bows running from front to back. The front seat wasn't your ordinary bench, nor was it a bucket. Split in three pieces, the outer sections swiveled out at the touch of a lever to aide easy entry and exit. Separated by a folding center armrest, the front could seat two, or with the armrest folded up, three. Swivel seats were standard on the Sport Fury (and DeSoto Adventurer and Chrysler 300E).

Completing the Sport Fury package was the custom nameplate shipped with each car reading, "Sport Fury Built Especially For ___ By Plymouth." Upon delivery the nameplate was to be en-

132

graved with the owner's name, then mounted on the glove compartment door. Topping off the interior was a special Sport Fury steering wheel with full-circle horn ring. The Fury and Belvedere wheels had a half ring, and the Savoy a horn bar integral with the spokes.

Fury interiors were as varied as the body styles. Hardtops got ivory hardboard headliners with ivory bows, sedans color-keyed cotton fabric. Sedan floors were covered in blue, green, brown, or gray carpet while hardtops had the additional choice of red carpeting. Hardtop seats received viscose-nylon Jacquard cloth in blue, green, brown, or gray with bolsters of color-keyed vinyl with pleated inserts. Sedans received the same seat upholstery with bolsters of harmonizing colors–door panels on hardtops simulated the seat fabric with Mylar and grained and pleated vinyls forming a five-tone pattern. Sedans used the same pattern with random-dot vinyl replacing the simulated fabric in the large panel.

The Belvedere convertible came in blue, green, brown, or gray ventilating vinyl with color-keyed bolsters of metallic-hued vinyl. Convertible door panels were also five-toned in grained and pleated vinyl and Mylar. Belvedere sedans and hardtops shared fabric-viscose Jacquard cloth in blue, green, gray, or tan with color-keyed bolsters; doors were finished in a three-tone pattern of grained and pleated vinyl. Savoy buyers had three two-tone color choices in nylon-viscose fabric, doors finished in block and grain sculptured vinyl forming a three-tone pattern. Savoy floors were covered with black rubber mats.

Even as the price leader the Savoy was dressed up much like its more expensive sisters. "There's no such thing as a 'Plain Jane' in the Plymouth line-up for 1959!" crowed the dealer data book. Standard equipment included the same front-end chrome, chromed taillights, windshield, and rear window moldings as top-line models. Also included were three-quarter length side moldings, two-tone instrument panel, turn signals, foam front seat cushion, dual sun visors, dual horns, and dual front door armrests. Optional Sportone trim was the same as used on the 1958 Silver Special, only now the spear rode higher on the body side. The Sportone trim provided a panel for a second color (painted to match the roof) in two-tone applications. Fury and Belvedere Sportone trim could be had with an anodized aluminum panel or be painted to match the roof.

Space age gadgetry added to the option list included an automatic headlight beam changer and "Mirror-Matic." The headlight changer, whose sensitivity was controlled by the driver (and overruled by the foot dimmer switch) automatically dimmed the headlamps when an approaching vehicle was 900–1200ft away. The system could also dim the

Special medallion on the Sport Fury was repeated on the grille, the tailfin, and the sportdeck hubcap. George Dalinis.

lights when following another car. Working on the same photoelectric principle, Mirror-Matic would adjust the inside rear-view mirror when a following vehicle's lights hit the photoelectric cell. Mirror-Matic was also driver controlled, choosing between "City" or "Highway" settings or "off."

Heavy-duty options for police and taxi fleets continued to grow. Such standard items as a 50amp generator, larger fuel tank (23gal capacity), Handy governor, heavy-duty clutch, springs, shocks, heavier seat springs, and high-compression economy head for the 6-cylinder continued to be offered. This year's package included special interior trim for the Savoy business coupe and all Savoy and Belvedere two- and four-door sedans, including two-tone gray vinyl upholstery with heavy-duty interior hardboard backing and heavy-duty floor mat. Taxis could also be ordered with dome lamp switches on all four doors, assist straps on "B" pillars, trip card for the left front door, rear door pull handles, Herculite side window glass, and floor pan sill ramps. Police vehicles could be factory wired for a roof light, including a pre-drilled hole in the roof. With its wide range of heavy-duty suspension and power options, Plymouth was clearly after the police car market. It had begun issuing special police car sales catalogs in 1957; by 1974 Plymouth would dominate the market, selling more police cars than any other auto maker.

The 1959 models ushered in a new serial numbering system, the second in as many years. Adopted corporate-wide, the system used ten digits. The first digit was the code letter "M," signifying the 1959 model year. The second numeral, using "1" for 6-cylinders and "2" for V-8s, indicated the type of engine (but did not designate *which* V-8 was installed). The third number in the sequence indicated model series, "3" signified Savoy, "5" Belvedere, "6" Fury, "7" station wagons (without designating series or differentiating between two- or four-door wagons). The fourth numeral indicated assembly plant, using "3" for Evansville, "4" for Los Angeles, "5" for Newark, "6" for Detroit, and "8" for Valley Park (St. Louis). The remaining six digits—all numerals—made up the sequential serial number, all beginning at 100,001.

Since 1946 the serial number plate had been riveted to the left front door post, but this, too, was changed for 1959. A new plate containing the serial number and other pertinent information including model number, body number, paint code, and schedule (build) date was mounted on the left side of the top cowl panel under the hood. Commonly known today as "fender tags," the data plate has since grown to include information on accessories in addition to the previous named data.

Road test results continued to put Plymouth in the forefront of the performance field. *Hot Rod, Mechanix Illustrated, Motor Life, Motor Trend, Speed Age,* and *Science & Mechanics* all tested cars equipped with the Golden Commando 395. In the popular 0–60mph dash *Hot Rod, Speed Age,* and *Science & Mechanics* all recorded a time of 8sec flat. *Mechanix Illustrated* did it in 8.2sec, and *Motor Trend* in 8.5sec. *Motor Life's* lead feet accomplished it in 7.8sec. The best any of the testers could do with the competition was a 9.9sec reading for a 352 Thunderbird-powered Ford and 10.1sec for Chevrolet's Super Turbo-Thrust 348ci triple-carbureted engine.

The Fury V-800 with Super Pak also put the competition in the weeds. *Motor Life,* testing a station wagon in its February 1959 issue, recorded 0–60mph in 10.5sec (top honors went to a 250hp Chevrolet Turbo-Thrust 348 V-8 at 10.3). Standard engines held their own as well. *Science & Mechanics* ran a Fury V-800 two-barrel 318 to the magic 60mph mark in 11.2sec. Chevrolet's 185hp 283 got there in 13.2sec, Ford's Thunderbird 292 arrived 1sec later.

Ride and handling continued to be strong points as noted by the same road test magazines. *Motor Life,* writing in the January issue: "Great handling car. Probably the best-handling sedan put out by Detroit since before World War II. May even surpass some sports cars." *Hot Rod* tested two

Nineteen fifty-nine marked the first time Plymouth had offered two convertibles in a single model year. The top of the line was the Sport Fury convertible. Owner: Gary Behling.

134

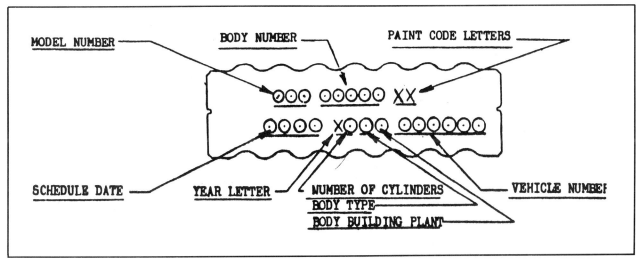

MODEL NUMBER — BODY NUMBER — PAINT CODE LETTERS

SCHEDULE DATE — YEAR LETTER — NUMBER OF CYLINDERS
BODY TYPE —
BODY BUILDING PLANT —
VEHICLE NUMBER

The new serial number system found identification numbers included with other pertinent data about the car, including (for the first time) paint code numbers. The data plate was located on the cowl under the hood.

cars for its November 1958 issue, one with air-level suspension the other with standard suspension, commenting, "ride and handling were excellent on both the test cars." *Motor Trend*'s January 1959 issue echoed the others saying, "Its firm road feel is comparable to a good sports car, an unheard of achievement with power steering."

As they had many times in the past, the federal government again passed legislation aimed at the auto industry. The Federal Automobile Information Disclosure Act took effect in 1959, requiring price stickers on all new cars. The window sticker had to show a vehicle's suggested retail price plus options and freight charges. Like the NADA used car price book, the window sticker changed the way dealers did business, remaining in effect to this day.

The 11 millionth Plymouth was built in March at Lynch Road, but the corporation was in the midst of a shake up, trying hard to keep Plymouth in third place and not quite knowing how to go about it. With 458,000 cars built during the model run, Plymouth had managed to hang onto its coveted third place. Ford and Chevrolet sales accounted for nearly half the new car sales in 1959. "A big reason is Plymouth's production and sales difficulties," commented *Motor Life*. In the same issue it also noted Plymouth's "quality is its weakest point—materials (are) not as good as competitors and assembly is inferior . . . " Despite the company's difficulties, Motor Life also commented, "The 1957-59 Plymouths will be pointed to in the years to come as 'great cars.' " Unfortunately, consumers also had concerns about Plymouth quality, and it would be eleven long years before the company would again see third place.

The pilot program begun earlier to separate Plymouth dealers continued. As the 1960 models began production, the number of Plymouth dealerships dropped from 6,308 to 4,138 mostly due to Dodge dealers giving up (many reluctantly) their Plymouth franchise. For the customer who was accustomed to visiting his local Dodge dealer to buy a new Plymouth, the move came as a surprise; few were the dealers who would let the customer walk out the door to visit another dealer. The instantly successful, low-priced 1960 Dodge Dart also hurt Plymouth sales.

A realignment of divisions July 1 found Plymouth and DeSoto combined into a single division (Chrysler and Imperial were combined into a second division, Dodge into a division of its own). This arrangement wouldn't last long. Having denied rumors of a compact car program for the past several years, Chrysler confirmed its existence May 21. Before the first car was built, Plymouth found itself with a new division name and a new mandate. August 8, 1959, saw the Plymouth-DeSoto division re-

Replacing the high-performance Fury was the watered-down Sport Fury series in either sport coupe or convertible. Owner: George Dalinis.

A tale of the tailfin, from start to finish. In the foreground is the 1956 "Airfoil," followed by the 1957–58 (1958 pictured) version, and the 1959 and 1960. Fins would disappear from Plymouths with the 1961 models. *Lanny Knutson.*

Not everyone cared for the finned 1959s. This Belgian-built seven-passenger sedan had the fins cut down considerably. The front fenders on this car are the 1958 design. This car was used by the late Shah of Iran during a royal wedding on the European continent. *Theo Huet.*

named Plymouth-DeSoto-Valiant Division of Chrysler Corporation. Powered by a tilted, overhead valve, in-line six, the Valiant would also rob sales from Plymouth.

Valiants began coming off the Dodge Hamtramck assembly line September 21. A "corporate" vehicle (ads boasting "It's Nobody's Kid Brother"), the first Valiants were not exclusive to Plymouth dealers; as late as January 1, 1960, less than half of Plymouth's 4,100 dealers were franchised to sell the car. It wouldn't be until 1961 that Valiant would become a "Plymouth."

The Valiant and Slant Six spelled a new era for Plymouth. As the last 1959 models were built, the doors at Evansville were closed for good, as it was replaced by the St. Louis plant, which hadn't quite made it on-line for the 1959s. There were other changes in the works as well. The Mayflower emblem, seen on every Plymouth except the 1958s, sailed off into the sunset, never to be seen again. The Slant Six replaced the venerable old flathead, ads for the new engine reading, "Out Of The Old Maid Class." An equally new method of building cars began as Plymouth—and Chrysler Corporation—switched to "Unibody" construction, in which the frame and body were one integral welded component, replacing body-on-frame construction used since the first Plymouth was built back in June 1928.

A new engine, a new method of construction, a new assembly plant—suddenly it *was* 1960, and the end of an era.

This Belvedere is another finless 1959. Its owner claims that Queen Elizabeth of Belgium ordered them cut off as she didn't like them. Owner: Wouter Schandevyl. *Collectible Automobile.*

Chrysler Australia used the U.S. 1953–54 body in Plymouth, Dodge, and DeSoto disguises until 1957 (and even later for the Chrysler Royal). Included in their production was the 1957 Plymouth UTE pictured here. Owner Robert Bloch.

Chapter 6

Gas Turbine Plymouths

"The car was moving under its own power. I was driving it and Sam Williams was sitting next to me. Dave Borden was in the back seat. Word had gotten out that we were going to try a turbine car for the first time. We started it and started to move out and the crowd cheered. It was quite an exciting event. There must have been 300 people hanging out of windows and leaning over the roof. With the cheers and the applause I suppose the rest of the place must have wondered what in the hell was going on over there. Word got around pretty fast. That was the fall of 1953." With those words, George Huebner Jr. recalled the first impromptu public showing of Chrysler Corporation's first gas

This 1954 Belvedere—here making its first trial run around Chrysler's Highland Park complex in October 1953—was the world's first production automobile powered by a gas turbine. *Chrysler Historical Foundation*

turbine-powered automobile as it was driven around Chrysler's Highland Park complex. The car, a white-over-beige 1954 Plymouth Belvedere two-door hardtop was not the first turbine-powered automobile in the world (Rover's Jet 1 held that distinction), but it did carry a distinction no car had to that time–it was the first *production* automobile in the world to be powered by a gas turbine.

Chrysler's turbine program dated back to World War II. In 1945, Chrysler had been issued a contract by the U.S. Navy's Bureau of Aeronautics to develop a turboprop engine. Work on an automotive version of the engine didn't begin in earnest until 1949 when the Navy contract ran out. Devel-

opment work consisted of improvements to the compressor, regenerator, burner controls, and other necessary gearing and controls needed to adopt a gas turbine to automotive use. Key obstacles were cost and materials availability; completely new tooling and manufacturing methods would have to be developed if a turbine engine was to be mass produced. Turbine engines, by their very nature, required special metal alloy and ceramic parts to withstand the extreme temperatures generated. Chrysler engineers were faced with two engine designs to choose from, either single- or two-shaft, and chose to develop the two-stage turbine (a gas generator stage and a power turbine stage).

Plymouth's third turbine car was this 1955 Turbine Special. Exterior changes included special hubcaps, ornamentation, and an exhaust outlet in the rear bumper. *Chrysler Historical Foundation*

In its simplest form, a turbine draws in air which is then compressed (and heated) before being subjected to mixing with fuel. In its first stage, the mixture is again compressed before passing on to the second or power turbine stage. Gas turbines were noted for extremely high exhaust temperatures, a problem Chrysler engineers solved by re-routing the exhaust gasses through rotating heat exchangers or regenerators. At the power turbine stage turbine blades could be operating at over 70,000rpm, a speed that had to be reduced through a series of reduction gears before power could be directed to a car's transmission.

News of Huebner's October 1953 test drive of the first turbine-powered production car wasn't released to the general public until March 25, 1954. With a mid-June dedication set for Chrysler's new Chelsea, Michigan, testing facilities, it was only natural that Chrysler would want to showcase its latest engineering developments during the ceremonies.

Chrysler engineers had begun to set up a 1953 Dodge sedan as the first turbine-powered car. With the fast approaching Chelsea dedication the switch to a more sporty Plymouth body style—at a time when Plymouth sales were lagging severely—was probably more of a public relations move than an engineering decision. Plymouth needed as much favorable publicity as it could generate even though the Chrysler Corporation gas turbine was just that—a *corporate* turbine rather than a Plymouth turbine.

The public got its first look at the Plymouth Belvedere Turbine when it was displayed at the Waldorf-Astoria Hotel in New York City from April 7 to 11. The Waldorf showing was a static display; it wouldn't be until the June 16 dedication ceremonies at Chelsea that the press and public would see and hear the turbine run, and then only in a series of "drive-bys" past the visitors' grandstands. Neither the press nor the general public would get a chance to get behind the wheel of the turbine car.

Measuring 32in long, 33in wide, and 28in high, the turbine, rated at 100hp, fit snugly into the Belvedere's engine compartment. Mated to a standard Plymouth transmission with only reverse and high gears, the turbine weighed some 200lb less

Turbine specials were not only made to go but to look good while on display. Although never publicly shown, under hood items were painted, padded, or chrome plated. Note the two 6-volt batteries. *Chrysler Historical Foundation*

than a conventional Plymouth 6-cylinder engine. Built essentially as a laboratory development tool, the first turbine, identified as the CR1, was considered by Chrysler engineers as a "milestone in automotive power engineering" because it embodied solutions to two of the major problems long associated with gas turbines: high fuel consumption and scorching exhaust gas. The key feature that contributed to removing these technical barriers was the heat exchanger or regenerator. Heat exchangers extracted heat from the hot exhaust gasses and transferred that energy back to the compressed air, thus easing the burners' job of raising gas temperature, conserving fuel, and lowering the exhaust temperature. At idle, the turbine's exhaust temperature

fell to 170deg Fahrenheit, ranging up to 500deg under normal operating conditions.

Unknown to nearly everyone was the existence of a second 1954 turbine-powered Belvedere sport coupe–this car without the heat exchanger feature. Plans had been made to show both cars, side by side, at the Chelsea dedication to demonstrate the difference between a turbine with heat exchanger and one without. The second car–appropriately painted fire engine red–nearly caught fire from the turbine's intense heat during a pre-dedication test, thus canceling the comparisons. Of the two turbine cars, the white-over-beige car was the one always seen in press releases. The red car, in a photo cropped to show the turbine engine, was shown in

Turbine Special emblems identified the car as something special. It was driven just once on city streets, on Good Friday, 1955. *Chrysler Historical Foundation*

color on the front cover of the August 1954 issue of *Motor Trend* (*Motor Trend* had published a two-page feature with the white-over-beige car in its May 1954 issue).

Everyone's question was, "When can I buy one?" James Zeder, Chrysler vice-president and director of engineering, replied, "Commercial production of gas turbines for passenger cars depends on long-range solutions to many complex metallurgical and manufacturing problems. There is no telling at this time how long it will take to solve these problems." Metals such as tungsten, cobalt, and molybdenum, necessary to the construction of a turbine, were costly and in scarce supply. "Plymouth's production line would drain the national supply in short order," Zeder continued.

With the exception of a 12in oval exhaust port beneath the rear bumper, the first Plymouth turbine cars appeared completely stock. George Stecher, who worked on Chrysler's turbine program for twenty-eight years, recalled another interesting aspect of the first turbine car. "The original '54 had no starter. We used to take an air motor–we had a T-handle bolted to the air motor, and we had a shaft that had a couple of tongues on it, and on the engine you had a shaft that had a couple of forks. And we used to sit there with it between our legs and start it that way. On shutdown, the soak-back temperatures got extremely high, so we used to have to sit there once we shut it down and continuously crank it, without feeding any fuel to it, just to cool the engine down so we didn't coke up the

The 1955 Turbine Special's instrument panel. Note the speedometer on the passenger side of the car; the odometer reads 238mi. *Chrysler Historical Foundation*

bearings and things of that sort. We had a lot of problems with that."

Almost a year later the same basic turbine engine was installed in a 1955 Plymouth Belvedere four-door sedan. Painted red and white, the 1955 Turbine Special carried a unique hood ornament and medallion, special body name plates and trunk medallion in addition to having an oval exhaust port built into the center of the rear bumper. The 1955 was never shown publicly but was driven on Detroit streets. Again, according to Stecher, "Any photographs you see of the car on the streets of Detroit–well, you'd have to go back to the calendar, but it was Good Friday, when they used to close places down from twelve to three. That's when we went out with a bunch of photographers, and we went to various gas stations and things of that sort. It was done for various publicity reasons, but never shown."

March 1956 saw Plymouth's third Turbine Special, an all-white Belvedere four door, take to the highway on the first cross-country test run of a turbine-powered automobile. Leaving New York City's Chrysler Building March 26, the car arrived four days and 3,020mi later in Los Angeles, California. Fuel economy on the trip averaged 13mpg, using mostly unleaded gasoline and diesel fuel (the turbine would burn any combustible liquid, from expensive French perfume to rot-gut whiskey). The trip was to be driven nonstop, with various drivers taking turns at the wheel. George Stecher, who drove on the first and last legs, recalled that the trip was not without its problems. A bearing in a reduction gear failed "due to somebody putting in a piece of copper tubing for an oil feed and it just fatigued and broke." Later a cracked intake casting was replaced. Chrysler was prepared for any trouble en route–the entourage included not only the turbine car but three station wagons and a truck carrying fuel, spare parts, and a complete spare engine.

Like the 1955 Belvedere, the cross-country car was modified only to the extent of having special

The turbine in the 1955 car was comparable in size and horsepower to Plymouth's new V-8, but lighter weight. *Chrysler Historical Foundation*

143

hood medallions, body name plates, and a modified rear bumper with exhaust port. The cross-country Turbine still used the first generation turbine engine, which had been further refined through the addition of automatic controls for turbine temperature, idle, and top speed.

Later in the year, a second 1956 Belvedere Turbine Special was built using a completely redesigned turbine dubbed the CR2. The CR2 was rated at 200hp, double that of the first version. This Belvedere was never publicly shown and lacked some of the distinctive features of the cross-country turbine. Both 1956 Turbine Belvederes were fitted with green interiors.

Turbine development work continued, with the engine installed next into a white 1957 Plymouth sedan. This turbine, also a second generation CR2 version, was never shown publicly and was later modified to look like the 1958 series Plymouths. Why Chrysler bothered to update the looks of the car remains something of a mystery—even today Chrysler's history of the turbine project fails to even mention the 1957–58 Turbine Special!

Following a public absence of nearly three years, Plymouth officially unveiled the CR2 turbine in a red 1959 Fury four-door hardtop. Like the original CR2 version in the 1956 and 1957–58 cars, this turbine was rated at 200hp. This car was taken out on the highway, logging a 576mi test run from Detroit to New York City and back in December 1958. This second generation turbine, also considered "just a laboratory tool," was improved in nearly all respects. Three major components, the compressor, regenerator, and burner, showed significant improvements in operating efficiency. At an average speed of 38mph, the turbine logged 19mpg on the run east—on the return trip, averaging 51mph, mileage dropped slightly to 17mpg. Fuel used on this trip included diesel fuel, JP4 jet fuel, and regular gasoline.

Chrysler engineer George Stecher prepares to take the 1956 Turbine Special on the first leg of its cross-country run. *Chrysler Historical Foundation*

By 1961 Chrysler engineers had again completely redesigned the turbine, referring to its third-generation turbine as the CR2A. First shown to the public in February 1961, the engine was installed in three different vehicles—a wildly designed show car called the Turboflite, a silver and red 1960 Plymouth Belvedere four-door hardtop, and a 1960

Dodge truck. Why these turbines weren't used in 1961 models was never explained. Later, a third-generation turbine would be fitted into a 1962 Dodge truck.

For whatever reason, Chrysler's next turbine-powered automobiles came from Dodge—a pair of 1962 Dodge Turbo Darts. One of the Turbo Darts,

George Huebner (right), father of Chrysler's turbine program, discusses mechanical aspects of the car with James Zeder, chief engineer. *Chrysler Historical Foundation*

a light blue two-door hardtop, was driven cross country by George Huebner, who left New York City on December 27, 1961, and arrived in Los Angeles on New Year's Eve.

Eventually the turbine engine found its way into a pair of 1962 Plymouth Fury hardtop coupes dubbed the Turbo Furys; the Turbo Furys, along with the Turbo Darts, began an extensive dealership tour in cities such as Los Angeles, San Francisco, Kansas City, St. Louis, Cleveland, Detroit, and Chicago to test consumer reaction. Tour schedules included first displaying the cars to members of the press, giving each newsman a ride in the car and staging special tests. Following the press conferences, the cars went on display. By the time the tests were finished, the cars had been shown in ninety cities in both the U.S. and Canada.

At each showing the question was asked, "If this car were offered for sale to the motoring public, do you think you would buy one?" Thirty percent answered yes, they would definitely buy one, with 54 percent answering they would seriously think of buying a turbine-powered car. Basing on these replies, Chrysler Corporation released a statement Valentine's Day 1962 that it would build "fifty to seventy-five turbine-powered passenger cars" that would be made available to selected users by the end of 1963. Three months later Chrysler unveiled

the Elwood Engle designed Ghia-bodied Turbine Car at the Essex House in New York City. On the same day a ride-and-drive program for the press was held at the 2-1/2mi Roosevelt Raceway Park on Long Island. Chrysler dealers got their first hands-on look at the car at the Waldorf-Astoria May 15.

With the switch to the semi-production Ghia Turbine Cars (fifty-five were built, fifty of which were used in Chrysler's Consumer Delivery Program, which ran from October 29, 1963, through January 28, 1966), Plymouth's involvement in Chrysler's turbine program began winding down. Two 1964 Turbine Plymouths were built, one powered by a "fourth generation" design, the other with a "fifth generation" turbine. The last Plymouth Turbine cars, a pair of Satellite sedans built in 1973, marked Plymouth's last efforts in the corporation's Turbine program.

What had begun as a serious attempt to produce an alternative to the piston engine automobile eventually fell by the wayside. Between 1953 and 1970 Chrysler invested $100 million of its own funds in the turbine program, with the U.S. government investing an additional $19 million between 1972 and 1980. The Arab oil embargo of 1973, Chrysler's declining fortunes in the late 1970s, and stringent government regulations all helped kill the

The 1957–58 turbine—modified here to reflect 1958 trim—was never seen in public. The only external difference over regular production cars was the exhaust outlet in the center of the rear bumper. *Chrysler Historical Foundation*

project. When the program was discontinued an eighth generation turbine was on the drawing boards, designed to be used with the K-car platform. When the axe fell, Chrysler Corporation had built a total of eighty turbine-powered motor vehicles–fourteen Plymouths, seven Dodges, two Dodge trucks, two dream cars, and fifty-five Ghia-bodied coupes.

None of the early turbine cars still exist. Considered merely prototypes and test mules, the cars were eventually scrapped.

Fate was slightly kinder to nine of the fifty-five Ghia Turbines. Because the bodies of these cars had been built in Italy, they were brought into the country under a Customs bond. Eventually Chrysler had the choice of paying duty on the vehicles or scrapping them–it chose the latter. The turbine engines were removed and the cars trucked to the "bone yard" at the Chelsea test facility where Chrysler prototypes are routinely cut apart. Under the watchful eye of Elmer Kiel, Chelsea's destruction overseer, the cars were pulled off the transporters, the hood and deck lids torched off, the windows smashed, and the interiors set on fire before the bodies were loaded into a crusher.

The remaining nine Ghia Turbines were dispersed to museums around the country. Chrysler Corporation retained three of the coupes, number

The 1959 Turbine Special was based on a Belvedere Sport Sedan. Special trim included a new grill, hubcaps, and orna-mentation. This car was driven from Detroit to New York City. *Chrysler Historical Foundation*

147

30, number 42, and number 47. The Harrah Collection in Reno, Nevada, got car number 31 which has since passed through the Domino Collection to Frank Kleptz, the only turbine car now in private hands. Car number 11 is in the National Museum of Transportation at St. Louis, car number 25 is in Detroit at the Detroit Historical Collection on Woodward Avenue, car number 34 resides in the Henry Ford Museum at Dearborn, and car number 44 at the Natural History Museum in Los Angeles. The last car, number 45, resides at the Smithsonian in Washington, D.C. Each car had to be shipped with the turbine disabled, but each was shipped with a fresh engine in a crate. Excepting the Chrysler-owned cars, all the cars remain inoperable. The Chrysler Historical Foundation possesses one of each of the seven generations of the turbine engine, reminders of Chrysler's valiant effort to mass produce a gas turbine-powered automobile.

Chrysler Corporation Turbine Car Production 1953–1980

Year, Make & Body Style	Number Built	Turbine Generation
1954 Plymouth Belvedere Sport Coupe	2	1
1955 Plymouth Belvedere 4-door	1	1
1956 Plymouth Belvedere 4-door	1	1
1956 Plymouth Belvedere 4-door	1	2
1957-58 Plymouth Belvedere 4-door	1	2
1959 Plymouth Fury 4-door hardtop	1	2
1960 Plymouth Fury 4-door hardtop	1	3
1960 Dodge 2-1/2ton truck	1	3
1961-2 Dodge 2-1/2ton truck	1	3
1961 Turboflite Show Car	1	3
1962 Plymouth Fury 2-door hardtop	2	3
1962 Dodge Dart 2-door hardtop	2	3
1963-66 Chrysler Ghia Turbine Coupe	55	4
1964 Plymouth (body style unknown)	1	4

The instrument cluster of the 1959 Turbine Special differed from standard production cars. In the left pod is a 160mph speedometer (odometer shows 2,023 miles). The right pod contains a 50,000rpm tachometer. In the center is a 2,000deg inlet temperature gauge. *Chrysler Historical Foundation*

Year, Make & Body Style	Number Built	Turbine Generation
1964 Plymouth (body style unknown)	1	5
1966 Dodge Charger Fastback	1	6
1966 Dodge Coronet 2-door hardtop	1	6
1973 Plymouth Satellite 4-door	2	6

Year, Make & Body Style	Number Built	Turbine Generation
1973 Dodge Coronet 4-door	1	6
1976 Dodge Aspen 4-door	2	7
1977 Chrysler "LeBaron" Show Car	1	7
1980 Dodge Mirada 2-door Coupe	1	7

George Huebner demonstrates the cool exhaust of the 1959 Turbine Special. *Chrysler Historical Foundation*

The fuel canisters on the display rack are labeled, from left to right:

60% GASOLINE 40% METHANOL	60% DIESEL 40% ISOPROPANOL	COAL DERIVED FUEL	BROAD CUT 100-540° F DISTILLATION	ETHANOL (DENATURED)	NON-LEADED GASOLINE

Previous page
Ghia of Italy built the bodies for fifty-five turbine-powered coupes, fifty of which were placed in the hands of 203 drivers in a unique "real-world driving" situation. The cars were painted Turbine Bronze with the exception of this car which was painted white and appeared in the 1964 movie *The Lively Set*. All but nine of the cars were later crushed, including the movie car. *Chrysler Historical Foundation*

Plymouth's last hurrah in the turbine program came when a pair of 1973 Satellite sedans were built. As evidenced by the test here, the turbine would burn anything combustible. *Chrysler Historical Foundation*

All of the early Plymouth turbine cars were eventually destroyed, along with all but nine of the Ghia-bodied turbines. Six Ghias were placed in museums around the country, and Chrysler re-tained three. This photo shows one of the remaining Ghias surrounded by five generations of turbines. *Chrysler Historical Foundation*

Appendices

Model Information

Vehicle Identification Numbers
The serial number is stamped on a plate located on the left, front door post. The serial number sequences indicated only the series/model and assembly plant information according to the following number sequences:

1946		Start	End
P-15S	Detroit	15154001	15206935
	Los Angeles	26000001	26003588
	Evansville	22042001	22053039
P-15C	Detroit	11496001	11643103
	Los Angeles	25000001	25009752
	Evansville	20165001	20185185
1947			
P-15S	Detroit	15206936	15252278
	Los Angeles	26003589	26010839
	Evansville	22053040	22063369
P-15C	Detroit	11643104	11854385
	Los Angeles	25009753	25035585
	Evansville	20185186	20233167
1948			
P-15S	Detroit	15252279	15284535
	Los Angeles	26010840	26017025
	Evansville	22063370	22071866
P-15C	Detroit	11854386	12066019
	Los Angeles	25035586	25062782
	Evansville	20233168	20287571
1949			
P-15S	Detroit	15284536	15292209
	Los Angeles	26017026	26018852
	Evansville	22071867	22073646
P-15C	Detroit	12066020	12116123
	Los Angeles	25062783	25071430
	Evansville	20287572	20299138

1949 Second Series 6(DeLuxe))

P17	Detroit	18000101	18040467
	Los Angeles	28000101	28003814
	San Leandro	28500101	28503162

1949 6(DeLuxe)

P18	Detroit	15300001	15358928
	Los Angeles	26025001	26030100
	San Leandro	26500101	26503423
	Evansville	22080001	22096252

1949 6(DeLuxe)

P18	Detroit	12120001	12384178
	Los Angeles	25075001	25097094
	San Leandro	25500101	25510640
	Evansville	20304001	20366486

1950

Deluxe P19	111in wb	
	Detroit	18041001 to 18119094
	Los Angeles	28004001 to 28009848
	San Leandro	28503501 to 28511177
	Evansville	24012001 to 24035538
	Windsor	95003001 to 95006710
Deluxe P20	118.5in wb	
	Detroit	15359501 to 15456084
	Los Angeles	26030501 to 26035870
	San Leandro	26504001 to 26510569
	Evansville	22097001 to 22125803
	Windsor	95504001 to 95508435
Special Deluxe P20	118.5in wb	
	Detroit	12384501 to 12627867
	Los Angeles	25097501 to 25110385
	San Leandro	25511001 to 25527262
	Evansville	20367001 to 20428448
	Windsor	96013001 to 96029393

1951

Concord P22	111in wb	
	Detroit	18126001 to 18192309
	Los Angeles	28011001 to 28015557
	San Lenadro	28513001 to 28518994
	Evansville	24042001 to 24056628
	Windsor	95007001 to 95009995
Cambridge P23S	118.5in wb	
	Detroit	15460001 to 15577561
	Los Angeles	26040001 to 26045620
	San Leandro	26512001 to 26518068
	Windsor	95509001 to 95513633
Cranbrook P23C	118.5in wb	
	Detroit	12635001 to 12906467
	Los Angeles	25112001 to 25125247
	San Leandro	25531001 to 25545962
	Evansville	20435001 to 20484924
	Windsor	96030001 to 96044454

1952

Concord P22	111in wb	
	Detroit	18192501 to 18223600

	Los Angeles	28015701 to 28018555
	San Leandro	28519101 to 28522352
	Evansville	24056701 to 24063833
	Windsor	95010001 to 95011211
Cambridge P23S		
	118.5in wb	
	Detroit	15577801 to 15662660
	Los Angeles	26045701 to 26049991
	San Leandro	26518201 to 26523546
	Evansville	22159601 to 22181520
	Windsor	95513701 to 95517134
Cranbrook P23C	118.5in wb	
	Detroit	12906701 to 13066238
	Los Angeles	25125301 to 25134190
	San Leandro	25546101 to 25555957
	Evansville	20485001 to 20516075
	Windsor	96044601 to 96057734

1953

Plymouth changed its method of applying serial numbers this year; the sequential number providing only information as to where the car was built. The serial number sequence no longer indicated the model/series information, (except Canada)
Cambridge P24-1 and Cranbrook P24-2

	Detroit	13070001 to 13505004
	Los Angeles	25136001 to 25161846
	San Leandro	25560001 to 25588345
	Evansville	20520001 to 20657000
Cambridge P24-1	Windsor	95517201 to 95523335
Cranbrook P24-2	Windsor	96057801 to 96072616
Belvedere P24-3 **	Windsor	96900001 to 96903000

** This car line was exclusive to Canadian production

1954

Plaza P25-1	Detroit	13506001 to 13829336
Savoy P25-2	Los Angeles	25163001 to 25175377
Belvedere P25-3	San Leandro	25590001 to 25606284
	Evansville	20658001 to 20739829
Plaza P25-1	Windsor	95524001 to 95528539
Savoy P25-2	Windsor	96073001 to 96088055
Belvedere P25-3	Windsor	96904001 to 96910880

1955

The serial number now indicated not only the plant of assembly but also indicated whether the car was powered by a 6–or 8–cylinder engine. Model series designations were NOT included in the serial number sequences.

6-cyl Plaza P26-1	Detroit	13835001 to 14119261
6-cyl Savoy P26-3	Evansville	20745001 to 20819358
6-cyl Belvedere P26-2	Los Angeles	2518001 to 25200109
6-cyl Plaza P-26-1	Windsor	95528601 to 95536300
6-cyl Belvedere P26-2	Windsor	96088101 to 96106850
6-cyl Savoy P26-3	Windsor	96800001 to 96801000
V-8 Plaza P27-1	Detroit	15663001 to 15871476
V-8 Belvedere P27-2	Evansville	22182001 to 22244749
V-8 Savoy P27-3	Los Angeles	26524001 to 26550290
	Windsor	96910901 to 96916775

1956

6-cyl Plaza P28-1	Detroit	14120001 to 14272723
6-cyl Savoy P28-2	Evansville	20820001 to 20857927
6-cyl Belvedere P28-3	Los Angeles	25202001 to 25212960
6-cyl Plaza P28-1	Windsor	95536401 to 95545250
6-cyl Savoy P28-2	Windsor	96107001 to 96123403
6-cyl Belvedere P28-3	Windsor	95999001 to 95999049

V-8 Plaza P28-1	Detroit	15873001 to 16080450
V-8 Savoy P29-2	Evansville	22247001 to 22325907
V-8 Belvedere P29-3	Los Angeles	26552001 to 26590897
V-8 Plaza P29-1	Windsor	95566501 to 95569750
V-8 Savoy P29-2	Windsor	91677101 to 96188637
V-8 Belvedere P29-3	Windsor	96916901 to 96921570

1957

(Starting serial numbers only available)

6-cyl Plaza P30-1	Detroit	14280001
6-cyl Savoy P30-2	Evansville	20860001
6-cyl Belvedere P30-3	Los Angeles	25215001
V-8 Plaza P31-1	Detroit	16083001
V-8 Savoy P31-2	Evansville	22330001
V-8 Belvedere P31-3	Los Angeles	26595001
6-cyl Plaza P30-1	Windsor	95545301
6-cyl Savoy P30-2	Windsor	96123501
6-cyl Belvedere P30-3	Windsor	95999101
V-8 Plaza P31-1	Windsor	95569801
V-8 Savoy P31-2	Windsor	96188701
V-8 Belvedere P31-3	Windsor	96921601

1958

Plymouth adapted a new system for serial number coding this year. The letters LP-1 indicated a 6-cylinder car while LP-2 indicated a V-8 car. The model code code L, M, and H were used to indicate a low-priced car, a medium-priced car, or a high-priced car. The serial number code also indicated the assembly plant.

6-cyl Plaza LP1-L	Detroit	LP1-1001 on up
6-cyl Savoy LP1-M	Evansville	LP1E-1001 on up
6-cyl Belvedere LP1-H	Los Angeles	LP1L-1001 on up
	Newark	LP1N-1001 on up
	Windsor	LP1W-1001 on up
V-8 Plaza LP2-L	Detroit	LP2-1001 on up
V-8 Savoy LP2-M	Evansville	LP2E-1001 on up
V-8 Belvedere LP2-H	Los Angeles	LP2L-1001 on up
	Newark	LP2N-1001 on up
	Windsor	LP2W-1001 on up
Fury LP2-S	Detroit	LP2-1001

1959

Plymouth adopted a new system of assigning serial numbers. This ten digit system indicated model year, engine, model series designation, assembly plant, and a six digit sequential serial number. This system went into effect Sept 12, 1958. The plate on the left, front door post was discontinued and a new plate containing additional information (paint codes, schedule date, etc) was mounted on the left side of the top cowl panel under the hood.

Serial number breakdowns for the 1959 models are as follows:
1st digit — Letter code "M" signifies 1959 model year
2nd digit — Number designation for car line —
　　　　　　　"1" for Plymouth 6-cylinder
　　　　　　　"2" for Plymouth V-8
3rd digit — Number designation for model series —
　　　　　　　"3" Savoy
　　　　　　　"5" Belvedere
　　　　　　　"6" Fury
　　　　　　　"7" All station wagons
　　　　　　　"8" Taxi
　　　　　　　"9" Sport Fury, police, & all
　　　　　　　　　special models
4th digit — Number indicates assembly plant —
　　　　　　　"3" Evansville, IN
　　　　　　　"4" Los Angeles, CA

5th thru 10th digits — Sequential serial number, all beginning at 100,001

Production Figures

1946-1949 P15
P15S Deluxe

Business Coupe	16,117
2 Door	49,918
4 Door	120,757
Club Coupe	10,400
Chassis	10

P15C Special Deluxe

Business Coupe	31,399
2 Door	125,704
4 Door	514,986
Club Coupe	156,629
Convertible	15,295
Station Wagon	12,913
Chassis	5,361

53,491 cars built with right hand drive; no P15S RHD built

1949

P17 Deluxe Business Coupe	13,715
2 Door	28,516
Suburban	19,220
Chassis	4
P18 Deluxe 4 Door	61,021
Club Coupe	25,687
P18 Special Deluxe 4 Door	252,878
Club Coupe	99,680
Convertible	15,240
Station Wagon	3,443
Chassis	981

1950

P19 Deluxe Business Coupe	16,861
2d	67,584
Suburban	27,910
Special Suburban	6,547
P20 Deluxe 4d	87,871
Club Coupe	53,890
P20 Special Deluxe 4d	234,084
Club Coupe	99,361
Convertible	12,697
Station Wagon	2,057
Chassis	2,091

1951-52
P22 Concord (wb 111in) 1952:

	Production
Business Coupe	14,255
Sedan 2d	49,139
Savoy	20,519
Suburban	56,001

P23 Cambridge (wb 118.5in)

Sedan 4d	179,417
Club Coupe	101,784

P23 Cranbrook (wb 118.5in)

Sedan 4d	388,785
Club Coupe	126,725
Convertible Coupe	15,650

Belvedere Hardtop Coupe	51,266
Chassis	4,171

1953
P24-1 Cambridge (wb 114in)

	Production
Business Coupe	6,975
Sedan 2d	56,800
Sedan 4d	93,585
Club Coupe	1,050
Suburban Station Wagon 2d	43,545

P24-2 Cranbrook (wb 114in)

Sedan 4d	298,976
Club Coupe	92,102
Belvedere Hardtop Coupe	35,185
Convertible Coupe	6,301
Savoy Station Wagon	12,089
Chassis	843

1954
P25-1 Plaza (wb 114in)

	Production
Business Coupe	5,000
Club Coupe	1,275
Sedan 4d	43,077
Sedan 2d	27,976
Suburban Station Wagon	35,937
Chassis	1

P25-2 Savoy (wb 114in)

Club Coupe	30,700
Sedan 4d	139,383
Sedan 2d	25,396
Suburban Station Wagon 2d	450
Chassis	3,588

P25-3 Belvedere (wb 114in)

Sedan 4d	106,601
Sport Coupe Hardtop	25,592
Convertible Coupe	6,900
Suburban Station Wagon 2d	9,241
Chassis	2,031

1955

Model & Body Style	6-cyl	V-8
Plaza 4d	68,826	15,330
2d Suburban	23,319	8,469
4d Suburban	10,594	4,828
Business Coupe	4,882	0
Club Coupe	45,561	8,049
Savoy 4d	93,716	69,025
Club Coupe	45,438	29,442
Chassis		0
Belvedere 4d	69,128	91,856
Club Coupe	19,471	22,174
Sport Coupe	13,942	33,433
4d Suburban	6,197	12,291
Convertible		8,473
Chassis		10

P26-4 Belvedere - All Six Cylinder (Canada only model)

Club Coupe	100
Sport Coupe	93
4d	786
4d Suburban	21

1956

Model & Body Style	6-cyl	V-8
Plaza Business Coupe	3,313	415
4d	44,628	15,569